# DENIS LAWSON

Denis Lawson has been an actor for over forty years and has worked extensively on stage, film and television.

His stage credits include *Bits of Lenny Bruce* (King's Head Theatre), and Joey in *Pal Joey, Mr Cinders, Lend Me a Tenor, Oleanna* and *La Cage aux Folles,* all in the West End.

Film credits include *Providence, The Man in the Iron Mask, Local Hero, Perfect Sense, Broken* and, most recently, *The Machine.*

Television credits include *Dead Head, That Uncertain Feeling, The Justice Game, Criminal Justice, Sensitive Skin, Bleak House, Marchlands, Inside No. 9.* He is currently in the series *New Tricks.*

Denis has directed three short films, *The Bassplayer, Solid Geometry* and *In the Mix.* On stage, he has directed *Little Malcolm and His Struggle Against the Eunuchs* (Hampstead Theatre and the Comedy Theatre in the West End), *Burning Issues* (Hampstead Theatre) and *The Anniversary* (Liverpool Playhouse and Garrick Theatre in the West End).

# Denis Lawson

# THE ACTOR AND THE CAMERA

Foreword by Ewan McGregor

Nick Hern Books
London
www.nickhernbooks.co.uk

A Nick Hern Book

*The Actor and the Camera*
first published in Great Britain in 2014
by Nick Hern Books Limited,
The Glasshouse, 49a Goldhawk Road,
London W12 8QP

Cover photo by Amanda Searle
Illustrations by Chris Wray (www.chriswray.co.uk)

Designed and typeset by Nick Hern Books
Printed and bound in Great Britain by
T.J. International, Padstow, Cornwall

A CIP catalogue record for this book is available
from the British Library

ISBN 978 1 84842 345 9

*For Sheila Gish*

*In memory of her extraordinary talent*

# FOREWORD

*Ewan McGregor*

'Walk forward and stop at the socks.'

It was the night before my first ever day on set. I had completed almost four years of theatrical training the week before, and I was standing in my uncle's bedroom facing him and the pair of socks that were lying on the floor at the opposite end of the room.

'What?' I said.

'Walk forward and stop with your feet just behind the socks,' said my Uncle Denis. I tried. 'No, don't look down at them. Go again.'

The next morning I was to begin six months of filming on *Lipstick on Your Collar*. My first job out of drama school. It was six one-hour episodes and I was to play Private Hopper. It was great good fortune to be given this amazing start to my career. I would get to be a cheeky, Cockney, bored music fantasist – and also get to play Elvis and Jerry Lee Lewis and Gene Vincent. I knew what to do with the character, sort of instinctively, but I had absolutely no idea of how to play him for a camera on a film set. How that all worked was a mystery.

So there I was with Denis and in an evening he taught me what he's about to teach you in this book. Who is who on a set. What you can expect. How to protect your work, your performance, from the technical distractions around you, in fact how to use them to your benefit. Wide shots, close-ups, eye-lines, marks, wild tracks – tips and pointers learnt in an amazingly varied and wonderful career.

This stuff is just not taught as part of an actor's training anywhere that I know and the knowledge in this book will arm the actor heading onto a set for the first time with an understanding of how it all works. That – with their excitement and passion – will give them a great deal of confidence and help them not to be overwhelmed and bamboozled by the sometimes hectic craziness that they find there.

My Uncle Denis has always been my acting hero and to this day still the only person in the world that I turn to when I get stuck or need advice about what I'm trying to do with a role. The masterclass Denis gave me that night helped me to get on with my job of playing Hopper right off the bat, and pretty soon to feel at home in front of the lens.

'Okay, you've got that, Ewan. Now throw a left-handed banana onto the socks.'

'What?'

# IMPORTANT NOTICE!
# PLEASE READ

This book is a summary of my forty-odd years in front of the camera, with some experience behind it and also on the production side.

It's *my* experience: what I've learned, what I practise. For those of you who are just starting off as actors, many of the ideas and my approach to particular challenges may be hard for you to deal with in the early stages of your career. Don't feel disappointed with yourself; most of the information in this book took me years to formulate, and years of confidence to practise.

I must stress that if anything I'm suggesting throws you in any way then discard it for the time being, and come back to it further down the line when you have more experience and confidence. Some of my approach (which is now a very technical one) may not suit you at all but the fact is: there is so little information out there about this vital part of our work that at the very least, you can use it as a springboard, a subject for discussion, to develop your own approach. Principally, I hope that it will help you arrive at your filmic destination a few years earlier than you might have done, that it will at least give you a starting point, a point of reference, to embrace or indeed to kick against.

*Denis Lawson*

# MY FIRST TAKE

When I was in my final year at drama school in Glasgow, I landed a role in *Dr. Finlay's Casebook*, a very successful television series at the time, starring the late Andrew Cruickshank and Bill Simpson and set in the thirties. I played a schoolboy who suffered from tunnel vision (no peripheral vision). So the first shot I ever did as a professional actor? I had to sit on the kerbside in a wee Scottish village in Perthshire, in shorts and tackety bits (big boots), and play with some stones. Bill Simpson drove a very large vintage car down a hill towards me. My instructions from the director were: when I thought (note the word 'thought') that the car was near enough to me, I was to run across the road right in front of it – I couldn't look at the car, I was supposed to judge when it might just miss me, then run! I did my first ever take. The director came over to me, 'That was a bit early. I don't mind if your hand goes onto the bonnet as you run in front of it.' Well, what did I know? I did it another couple of times, I got it in the can and I'm still here! How would I handle that now? Well, in these days of health and safety, it would never arise, but if it was requested, I'd say to my director, 'Sure, show me with the car just exactly what you want me to do.' Or to put it more succinctly, 'You must be fucking kidding.'

Starting out, as I did, in the early seventies, there were plenty of provincial theatres that you could go to, to do a season of plays for, say, six to nine months; rehearsing and playing constantly; putting on a new play every two or three weeks (at that time even weekly rep was still around here and there); playing parts that you were perhaps not best suited to (in other words, being able to fail) and generally finding your feet technically and emotionally. There were also ample opportunities for much more avant-garde work on the fringe, where you'd find companies challenging accepted norms of performance, with plenty of success and failure.

For the contemporary actor, emerging into the glare of the profession today, these theatrical opportunities have shrunk considerably. The result of all this is that a British drama student, who has spent three years working his or her arse off and has been given what is arguably one of the best stage trainings in the world, is more likely leave that institution and walk in front of a camera, and not onto the stage. Maybe they'll do a couple of days on *EastEnders* or *Casualty*, maybe they'll be whisked straight into a lead in some major movie or television series (the camera and the modern industry has an insatiable appetite for young faces).

It's taken most drama schools quite some time to wake up to how radically the profession has changed over the last twenty years or so, but they are now trying to get to grips with this side of an actor's training.

Having looked at the range of options in various schools, I would say, at this point in time, that they are tackling this with varying degrees of success.

Present courses seem to be run mostly by directors. Of course, a director's viewpoint is entirely valid, but it's a very different view from an actor's perspective, when it comes to dealing with the vagaries of a film set. I'm sorry to say that I spent a day not too long ago in a very well-established drama school and was shocked by some of the 'advice' the students had been given by a director.

I'd certainly encourage the inclusion of experienced actors into the mix and, where possible, experienced technicians. It took me many years of work to feel able to cross-examine a Director of Photography about his work and the workings of the camera, and to get into the editing suite after the shoot. It would be a great gift to give students that opportunity before they get out into the business.

I guess the catalyst for this book (and for quite a lot of other things) came from a movie I was in called *Local Hero*. We were shooting on the beach one day. I was standing beside the camera, doing off-lines, hugging the lens for my fellow actor (I'll explain that further down the line). The camera crew were reloading the camera (putting in a new reel of film). The clapper loader and focus puller were busy with this intricate task, which they'd repeated a thousand times; it was all automatic to them. I was staring at this black box and I realised I knew nothing about it, how it functioned, its inner workings: but this was where my performance was going. Down the lens. Into what? What? How?

That moment, on that beach, has driven me to this one. I decided to learn as much about the film-making process as I could, so that I could be more effective in front of this mysterious piece of machinery. It's been a long, drawn-out process and a fascinating one, which eventually turned me into a film-maker myself – and curiously also into a stage director. I still have plenty to learn but the endless fascination of this job (a weird way to make a living by anyone's standards) is that you never quite arrive, you're always pushing to get there.

This book is basically a technical one, to do with the way an actor functions within the lumbering animal that is the film unit. Hopefully it will give you some clues as to how to deal with that animal, how to use it to your best advantage to get what you need from it, to help you do a better job. How to sit in the centre of the unit, when all that frantic activity finally quietens down and the focus moves on to you, the actor – and essentially (and here's the big secret) to feel relaxed in the centre of the unit; to feel at home in front of the lens so that it always feels easy and never strained.

I'm throwing in some lifemanship – how I approach my work and the situations that arise from it – which you can take or leave. Acting is, after all, a deeply personal business: your approach is your own; you are unique to yourself and that is how it should be. Don't trust anyone; always question either outwardly or inwardly. I am deeply suspicious of anyone who maintains that they can somehow 'teach' you to act, or worse, can lead you towards your 'emotional life' as an actor. This book is essentially information, and as an actor who attended one of my workshops said: 'information is power'. I hope that sense of empowerment will quite simply help you to *enjoy your work*! We all signed up to do this weird acting thing because we have a vocation and are passionate about it, but it seems to me, that, of course, we're stressed when we're out of work but a lot of the time we are also stressed when we're *in* work! I love this side of my work, getting onto a set and working with a crew gives me such a buzz; largely because I understand the process I'm involved in and therefore feel totally at ease in that environment. The purpose of this book is to help you understand it and therefore love it too. The more you know, technically, about film work, the less you will feel at the mercy of the unit (that film-making machine). You'll begin to achieve relaxation in front of the lens, feeding it, giving it, and thereby giving the director and the editor, the material they need to create that polished final cut. Hopefully you'll walk away at the end of a day or when you're finally wrapped, feeling that you've got the best result out of the whole process and therefore achieved the best possible performance for yourself.

I trained at the Royal Scottish Academy of Music and Drama in Glasgow. We were fortunate enough to have our own multi-camera television studio, and we were involved in about three different productions on camera, while the technical students had experience behind the cameras, at the mixing desk, etc. Now this was all very useful and certainly helped with my early jobs, but... but: no one at any time discussed how to approach this side of our work, so that through my early years with the camera, questions kept formulating in my head.

- 'Is there a difference between the stage and the camera, in the way I pitch the performance both vocally and in intensity?'

Here was a real nagger:

- 'Do I find the camera, or do I let the camera find me?' (i.e. 'Do I just give a performance and ignore the camera?')

- 'Is there a difference between a wide shot and a close-up? Again in the pitch, the intensity of the way I play?'

- 'How do I cope with shooting a script completely out of sequence, even within scenes sometimes?'

- 'How do I sustain shooting a two- or three-page scene over a period of six, seven, maybe eight hours?'

- 'Is there a difference in my approach to the text from a play to film script?'

- 'Is there a difference in my fundamental approach to the character from stage to film?'

- 'Is there a difference between television and movie acting?'

- 'Is there a difference between television drama and sitcom in front of a live audience?'

Not only were these questions, and many others, not addressed at drama school, they were never even posited as ideas. Now, I am not being disloyal to the school that trained me: I'm convinced that these kinds of questions remain unanswered, even today, in most acting institutions.

In retrospect, I feel that, because none of these issues were raised in my training, it took me several years on film sets to piece it all together; a slow process because, first of all, as a young actor you don't want to look like an idiot, and secondly no one has the time on a unit to sit down and explain. In any event, you're coming from such a state of ignorance that you don't really know what the questions should be in the first place!

Oh... I'm still searching for a few answers.

Questions, though, are how you progress; finding more searching questions to ask, particularly of yourself; your own internal dialogue as an actor.

By the way, I will use the term 'film' in the book as a generic one, covering movies, television, traditional film cameras and all forms of digital cameras as well.

# CLASSICAL TO JAZZ

On stage we take great notice of the text; we want to be entirely accurate with it, to serve the play and the author to the best of our abilities, as a classical musician would with the score. We think about emphasis and phrasing to help project the emotional journey we want to take our audience on, as a classical musician might do. Rehearsals are a carefully structured process, with the director and the actors, as with the conductor and the orchestra. In both mediums a strong technique is essential and invariably demonstrated. However, in film, as with jazz, rehearsals can be minimal and there is less emphasis on 'placing' the text/music. What I'm getting at here is that, in film work, accuracy in the text can sometimes be secondary to spontaneity and character.

One of the most famous jazz albums ever made is called *Kind of Blue*, recorded in 1959 by Miles Davis and his quintet. If you don't know it and are sufficiently interested, it's very easy to get hold of. It's an absolute classic. On the day of the recording, Davis brought in the chord structures for the pieces. None of the musicians had seen anything of them. They played through them twice and then recorded what you hear on that album. For me, this is the most sublime 'chamber music', which I'd rather hear than any number of Mozart quartets – yes, sacrilege, I know! But these musicians were improvising together as a seamless team, working off the top of their heads, flying by the seat of their collective pants, like a cast of brilliant movie actors taking off from the text with only that rehearsal on the floor, on the day, then shooting/ recording.

Let's drop into this team of fabulous players and push into a close-up on the piano player, Bill Evans. Evans straddles both sides of my argument. He was a classically trained musician, who became so enamoured of jazz that he left his formal training behind to embrace the disciplines of improvisation. This is a quote from an interview with him:

> The simple things, the essences, are the great things, but our way of expressing them can be incredibly complex. It's the same with technique in music. You try to express a simple emotion... love, excitement, and sadness... and often your technique gets in the way. It becomes an end in itself when it should really be only the funnel through which your feelings and ideas are communicated. The great artist gets right to the

heart of the matter. His technique is so natural it's invisible or unhearable. I've always had a good (technical) facility, and that worries me. I hope it doesn't get in the way.

Demonstrating stage technique on camera is an absolute disaster; actually, to my mind, demonstrating stage technique on stage is a disaster too.

When I read this statement by Bill Evans, I realised that I'd gone through a very similar journey myself: shedding my stage technique, working against how I'd been trained for the stage. For instance, risking not being heard, losing all sense of 'projecting'; speaking even more quietly than I would do in life; throwing lines away; not driving them through to the end but letting them simply trail away. Flattening my delivery, not colouring the lines, as you might do for the stage. At one time (and this is a tricky suggestion), I experimented with not necessarily knowing the lines that well so that there was no danger of pressing too hard on the text – so that it seemed to slip out, without me thinking about it too much.

There's a wonderful movie called *Sweet Smell of Success*, starring Burt Lancaster and Tony Curtis, made in 1957, by the British director Alexander Mackendrick. The script was written by the celebrated American playwright Clifford Odets. Here's a note from Odets to Mackendrick: 'My dialogue may seem over-written, too wordy, too contrived. Don't let it worry you. You'll find that it works if you don't bother too much about the lines themselves. Play the situations, not the words. And play them fast.' I've only just come across this quote, but in many circumstances in my film work, that's exactly what I've been pursuing.

It was one of the old dames of the theatre who talked about 'jumping from emphatic word to emphatic word'. I was working against that principle, so that a deep naturalism evolved, ultimately rooting the character in me. I was not playing a 'character': the character was me; working against the notion of 'performance', certainly not seeming to give one. A good example can be found in comedy. When on stage, you would time a line for a laugh (feed line – beat/pause – laugh line – you hope!). Pushing against that formula on camera, you throw that laugh line away, risking not getting it, not giving a 'comic' performance but still being funny, by accident, or so it seems. It's more challenging, that's for sure. For me, comedy is the toughest of the disciplines, particularly on camera, where you have no audience to reassure you that you are actually being funny. I guess what happened is that I developed another technique, a 'camera technique'.

Here's another interesting quote about another wonderful musician on that same Miles Davis album, the tenor sax player Cannonball Adderly:

> His great technical facility perhaps stood in the way of his developing into a major jazzman. But he could not have found a better way to evolve as a musician than playing with Miles Davis. Nobody had a better understanding than Davis of how to make musical statements with economy of notes. This is not an easy thing to learn. Many musicians have said that the important thing about improvising is knowing what not to play. It takes time and great patience to discover this truth. Some critics have pointed out that Davis seemed to have the ability to edit complex lines as he played, reducing them to their essentials and implying more than he actually stated.

This is another very strong idea for us to look at. The ability, the confidence, to do *nothing*. To be still, to imply by understatement what you mean, to merely think it and the camera will know it. You can take these ideas back onto the stage, and they can be very powerful. The late, great Robert Mitchum said: 'Simplest is best.' He also described his job as: 'Turn up,

11

kiss the girl, take the money, go home.' It's a job: don't mystify it, keep it direct. He also said: 'Point the suit at the camera.' Which is perhaps a little too minimalist, even for me. I certainly feel that if I'm pushing and straining for something, it's wrong. It's what we don't show the camera that draws it to us, what we imply as an undercurrent, that can be so powerful. Again, that can apply to the stage too.

The television series *The Thick of It*, with my old pal Peter Capaldi, has elements of what I've just described. Normally you'd expect scripts three or four weeks ahead of shooting (although late scripts on television series are common, believe me) but here, the actors don't see the script for an episode until the readthrough. Once they've read it, they then improvise each scene, with the writers in attendance; this contributes to the rewrite of the script, which the actors get two days before filming. Once they have a scripted version of a scene in the can, they then do an improvised version. It's not uncommon for the actors to receive new speeches the night before and sometimes even hours before. You can see how the documentary style they achieve is helped by an enforced lack of preparation: because they're still fighting to be on top of the material on the actual takes. This is an unusual approach in television, but it has a great deal to do with the spontaneity of performance that I'm trying to describe and that I'm constantly looking for.

The movie *Tinker Tailer Soldier Spy* was released as I was writing this, and I came across this quote from Gary Oldman (who played George Smiley): 'Sometimes in a film it's like rock 'n' roll, you've got to burn with the first bar. Smiley's like jazz. I can build to that solo.'

There are certainly opportunities to improvise on the takes themselves. In fact, you should be working towards that kind of freedom in front of the lens when you have the confidence to try something out, without constant reference to the director. I will quite often ask a director not to shout 'Cut!' at the end of a take if I feel that I might have something to add, knowing that, if they don't like it in the edit, they can cut it – that's fine by me: I'm giving them options, they can take them or leave them. I've known instances of directors who won't shout 'Cut!' at the end of a take but will leave you to improvise out of it and will be picking up shots of the actors even when the dialogue is finished. In these cases, you just stay relaxed and in character for as long as you can stand it and break it yourself if it becomes too dull for you.

# STAGE TO FILM

Right: we're a bunch of actors in a room. We decide to put on a play.

We could achieve that goal without a script, without a director, without a set, without costumes, even without a venue... Oh yes we could. We could evolve a script in rehearsals through improvisation. We could direct each other; it's been done before. We could perform without lights, in street clothes, with no venue; we could perform in the street or a park! All we need is an audience, even if it's a couple of winos and a dog. Christ, some of my early experiences in the theatre were not far off that! One of my early jobs was to improvise a musical from an American novel, in ten days, with no musicians, singing snatches of famous musical numbers, unaccompanied. In the middle of rehearsals, two detectives walked into rehearsals, arrested the director (we were in Glasgow) and flew him to London, handcuffed, for what turned out to be a traffic offence. Meanwhile we carried on directing each other, doing some very good work by the way, until the director was released and returned three days later. The production was a great success.

But you can't make a film without a camera, and unless you're making a silent movie, you need some way of recording sound, so you are immediately involved in an intensely collaborative process with technicians. Over the last few years there has been a major technological upheaval in the industry, and there are certainly recent cases of independent films being made in quite a radical way. It is now possible to go off with a very small digital camera and just make that film. The director could shoot and edit him or herself on a laptop using current software, but, from our standpoint, even at that stripped-down, basic level, it's a very different experience. We are dependent on those pieces of machinery and the personnel who operate them to record our performance – and the better we understand that machinery and those personnel, the more comfortable we will feel in that environment and the more effective we will be.

Being in a rehearsal room with a director for anything from three to twelve weeks (personally, the most I've had is six) can be a hugely enjoyable, constructive experience. With film work, there can be little or no rehearsal, and that's where the discipline of private preparation comes into play: making all of those character decisions for yourself; having the self-confidence to make them, with no one sitting on your head (as in those theatrical rehearsals) you carry your own thoughts out in front of the lens. Of course there's direction, but it's instantaneous and on the moment. I've heard film work described as capturing the best of a rehearsal; that's not a bad way of looking at it. I've also heard it said that film is a director's medium; that the actor has no control. But you often have to fight for that control in the theatre, with a director breathing down your neck for weeks so that you end up in front of the audience with someone else's thoughts in your head, with rhythms and timings that are against your own instincts. And the director can still get at you when you come off! On film there's a sense that you've been employed to do a job, and that you turn up and do it. I find that tremendously liberating.

I was once involved in blocking a scene on film with an actress who tried to rehearse it like a play; she would say things like, 'I don't feel that I would move here,' or, 'I want to make that move across to the desk on that line.' The director replied, 'But I can't shoot the scene if you make those moves.' There is no argument with this, he's talking about technical considerations: it's logistically impossible in terms of camera moves and very possibly lighting requirements to do certain moves on a set. On stage it's critical for the actor to be placed effectively within the frame of the set (as a director in the theatre I consider that one of my chief functions for my actors), but generally on a film set I really don't mind where I am because all that matters is the shot. Is the shot interesting? Is the light good? Lighting is everything!! Give me a tasty light to work in and I'm happy; if I need to be one or two feet to my right to hit a light – baby, I'll be there! On *Bleak House*, I worked with the fabulous Director of Photography, Kieran McGuigan, and he was pointing out a small spotlight to me on set one day that would catch me when I hit my mark. I said, 'Don't worry, Kieran, I'll find it.' He looked at me as though demonically possessed, his Ulster accent rising to fever pitch, 'No! Don't *find* the light, Denis! *Love* the light! LOVE THE LIGHT!!' This is such a filmic point of view: you are working towards the shots, and great shots are brilliantly lit. To be frank, working in good light is sexy as fuck.

My antennae are also permanently out for theatrical moments: if anything I'm doing or been asked to do feels 'theatrical', I'll want to avoid it. The last thing I want is to look like I'm 'acting'. I'll often say, 'This feels a bit stagey,' and find another way round it. Maybe it's a move or a head-turn on a particular line, or just when I lift my eyes in a close-up that feels too emphatic, so I'll cut it back, move/lift my eyes in a less obvious way so that it doesn't look 'placed' but stays 'accidental'. This, again, is an element of film work I love: Michael Caine described it as 'working with a scalpel'. Making decisions about where you place your eyes in a shot, when you lift them, where you look and when, become the consideration: what you might do with a hand or an arm on stage, you indicate with your eyes in the frame.

# THE BASIC WORKINGS OF THE FILM CAMERA

The basic workings of the movie camera haven't changed in well over a hundred years. Louis Le Prince made one of the first cameras in 1888. It still exists in the National Media Museum in Bradford.

In 1889, the Englishman William Friese-Greene invented a camera that shot at ten frames a second on celluloid, but it was the Lumière Brothers in 1895 who organised the first commercial screening of ten short films at The Grand Café in Paris to a paying audience, thereby creating this monster of an industry. Each film was seventeen metres long, running through a projector for roughly fifty seconds. One of the films was called *La Sortie de l'Usine Lumière à Lyon* (or '*Workers Leaving the Lumière Factory in Lyon*') and ran for forty-six seconds.

I talked earlier about 'the mystery' of the film (movie) 35mm camera; so let me demystify that for you now. Here are the inner workings of the camera from an actor's perspective, i.e. not too technical!

Film stock (the term used for the film itself) comes in various sizes: 8mm, Super 8, 16mm, Super 16, 35mm and 70mm. It is made up of frames, with small perforations down each side.

8mm and Super 8 were used for home movies (before digital cameras came on the scene). 'Super' denotes that each individual frame is a slightly larger version, i.e. they've pushed the frame outwards, taking up more of the stock.

Super 16 used to be what most television drama was shot on (not soaps or long-running series). It has now all but disappeared. High-definition (HD) has replaced it. It was also used to shoot some low-budget features, *My Beautiful Launderette* and *Truly, Madly, Deeply*. It can be blown up into a 35mm print for cinema projection and has a nice 'grainy' look to it. 35mm is what most feature films were shot on, but more and more are now on HD. Most American television used to be on 35mm but HD has taken over there too.

70mm, which was known as 'CinemaScope', gives a fantastic image for a seriously epic movie, great for figures in a vast landscape, think *Lawrence of Arabia*.

Let's delve into the film camera, 16 and 35mm.

A reel of stock comes in a can:

• on 16mm it lasts 10min 40secs

• on 35mm, 11mins 6secs

The clapper loader, loads the reels of film into the can and claps each take with the clapperboard. They have to keep track of the amount of film, in feet, that is left in each reel – there's a small counter on the side of the camera. It can be infuriating if you start a take and run out of film halfway through. I'm glad to say it's very rare.

The stock is threaded through and around a cog system by the focus puller: there's a two-pronged hook, which takes hold of the stock, using the perforations on each side.

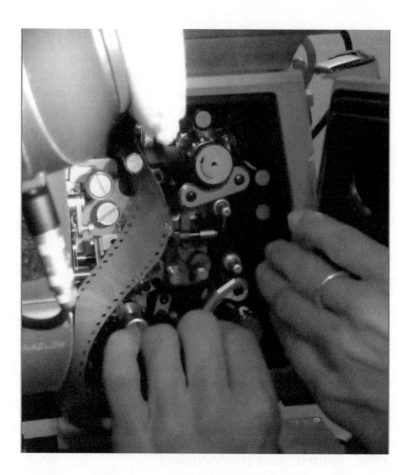

As the camera rolls (you can see where these terms originate), the motor in the camera pulls a frame in front of the gate, and that single frame of film is exposed, in exactly the same way that you'd take a still photograph (in a non-digital camera). But this happens in the film camera twenty-four times a second, so when you are in front of the lens, a still photograph of you is taken every 24th of a second. On television, it's twenty-five times a second, this is to do with the way that television broadcasts the image.

You are quite literally creating frames. When the exposed film is developed and run through a projector, it looks as though you're actually moving! It's as basic as a flick-book: the principle of making a series of drawings on a notepad, and then when you flick through them at speed, it looks as though your doodles are moving.

There are occasions when the speed of the stock through the camera is altered. If you want a slow-motion effect you run the stock faster through the camera, the actual speed depending on just how slow you want the image to look. 48 or 50fps (frames per second) is fairly normal for slow motion, but you can get cameras that will run at anything from 96fps to 3000fps to give you extreme slow motion.

Here's a specific example: if you roll a ball across a tabletop and it takes three seconds shot at 25fps, if you then shoot it at 50fps, it will take six seconds to roll across; at 100fps it will take twelve seconds, and at 300fps, thirty-six seconds.

In modern film cameras you have the ability to go in and out of slow motion without stopping the camera. The American director Michael Mann used this to great effect in *The Insider*. HD cameras have this facility now too.

As I began to understand the process, I developed a real sense of where my performance was going, down the lens and onto the emulsion on the film stock; as each frame is exposed, I'm burning myself into it. *This is my audience.* When I'm on stage it's those rows of people sitting in the dark, but here in front of the camera it's that lens, and the stock, humming over the cogs, past the gate, twenty-four times a second.

The romance of that image has been shattered somewhat by the arrival and development of high-definition cameras. HD cameras are basically computers, with menus and settings, the whole notion of gates, shutters, stock and cogs has gone. Your image is going down the lens onto a disk that can give you up to fifty minutes of recording time, and that disk is much,

much cheaper than film stock. In fact, now it's often going directly onto the hard drive in the camera.

When HD cameras first came out, they were cumbersome, expensive, and DOPs were not happy with them, but over the last ten years or so they've been improved at a dramatic rate. My experience over the last three years or so is beginning to swing me round to this new technology. The majority of movies are still shot on 35mm, but inroads are being made by HD all the time, and I can see a time when film stock will become like vinyl.

# THE DIFFERENCE BETWEEN HD AND FILM

Film has an atmosphere, a depth and a grainy quality that you have to work hard at to achieve on HD, where you tend to see every detail in a shot and even distant objects are clear, whereas on film they're soft in focus and there's more light and shade. HD is very good at shooting low lights, e.g. interiors or exteriors at night. Michael Mann used it in the feature *Collateral*, a great deal of which was shot at night, but for my money it had a terrible 'video' (flat) look to it in some scenes, and the atmosphere of the piece suffered as a result. HD deals less well with highlights, however. You might notice on television that if they are shooting towards a window and it's day, the window will seem very white and bright. This is still a defect with HD, this 'burning out' of highlights, although it is improving all the time.

For us actors it is pretty unforgiving: it will show every blemish, crease and bag! Make-up artists have to be very careful because HD can also emphasise make-up. You may find some of them using a little spray gun to apply make-up. It can feel a little odd to feel yourself being 'spray-painted', a bit cold and tickly, but it's worth it: it gives a flawless finish, and you're safe from that prying HD eye. HD has also had an impact on set design. They have to be very careful with purpose-built sets, as HD will spot any joins, false brick walls, painted backdrops, etc.

If you're a fledgling film-maker, I bet you could find yourself a free 16mm camera with free stock thrown in, since more and more of them will be gathering dust on shelves while HD continues its relentless progress. Working on a four-parter called *Marchlands*, I was fascinated as the DOP lined up a very close shot on a newspaper I was reading in the scene: he was using what looked like a small stills camera. I asked him if he was just getting a frame size for the shot, and he said, no, he was going to actually shoot the close-up with this small camera. I assumed that it wouldn't match the footage that we'd shot on the full-sized HD camera, and was amazed when he told me that it would match perfectly, with no extra work in the post-production process. Relentless progress indeed.

Since then I've worked with a couple of directors who have brought a small HD camera onto the set and picked up their own hand-held shots during takes.

Here are some productions on HD that I've been involved in that have really surprised me by the quality of the pictures:

- *Bleak House*, DOP Kieran McGuigan
- *Criminal Justice*, DOP Tat Radcliffe
- *Marchlands*, DOP Lukas Strebel
- *The Machine*, DOP Nicolai Brüel

And a couple of productions that I've not been in: *Top Boy*, directed by Yann Demange, DOP Tat Radcliffe, was exceptional in the way they embraced and used

HD to make a stylistic statement, as did the Swedish/Danish co-production *The Bridge* (the first season), DOP Jørgen Johansson.

# FILM MOTION

Because a film camera proper shoots at twenty-four frames a second, when we watch it as an audience (without being aware of it) we are actually watching a 'flickering' image, an image that is interrupted twenty-four times a second; this gives the movie image more weight and texture. As a kid we would often refer to the cinema as going to the 'flicks', now I understand why.

The digital image is completely smooth and flat and can seem a bit dull to the eye since we've been schooled in that more weighty film motion. Not to be outdone, the HD camera now has a function that will automatically interrupt that image twenty-four times a second, to give that movie feel, or indeed any other speed that's required. It can create the appearance of frames.

# THE SIZE OF THE IMAGE

Should there be a difference in your performance from television to feature films? I honestly don't think so. Okay, you're dealing with a huge image in a cinema and a much smaller one on television (although, with most people having wide screens at home these days that image is getting larger), but television generally uses a lot more close-ups than movies, where a close-up makes literally such a big statement that you have to be more selective with them. There are plenty of exceptions, of course. In the movie *Black Swan,* for instance, the camera was very close to the actors most of the time, creating a claustrophobic atmosphere for its story of intense emotions in the ballet world.

Michael Mann (*Heat* and *The Insider*) has a tendency to use more close-ups in his films than most, and I wonder if that's because he started in television. In any event, close-ups in television can be quite intense and extreme, and you have to learn stillness in either medium. I think a big mistake in a movie is to feel inhibited in your performance; the feeling to work towards is confidence, concentration and relaxation. There's a danger that you'll worry about the size of the movie image and get stuck; afraid to move your eyes or blink. Far better to forget all that and *enjoy yourself* in front of the camera, revel in the feeling of being in front of the lens. That goes for television too.

I remember a comment from an actor who now only does movies but started in television. 'I wouldn't work or perform in a different way if I were to do television again.'

Another difference between television and features is that television is dialogue-driven and a feature is highly visual. You'll see pages of stage directions in a feature-film screenplay that would be more unusual in a television drama. Again, there are exceptions: a lot of French cinema (the French love language), and Quentin Tarantino's movies are unusually dialogue-heavy for such commercially successful American features.

# MORE MONEY, MORE TIME

One of the main differences between television and movies, apart from the size of the image, is money and therefore time. If you were shooting a ninety-minute television drama, you'd probably have three weeks to shoot it. At the moment on the BBC, for instance, for a sixty-minute drama, you'd have a budget of around £700,000, going up to £900,000 for a period piece (period is always more expensive). It is roughly a minute of screen time to a page in a script. You'd normally have ten days to shoot a sixty-minute drama, so you're shooting around six pages a day. Doesn't sound that tough? Well, actually, you're working pretty fast to achieve this; everyone is.

On a properly funded feature the average is around two pages a day so everyone has more time – time for every department to get the best job done. More time for the prep (the period before the shoot), for the shoot itself and for post (the edit, etc.). More time to light the scenes, more time for intricate camera moves, more time for coverage (i.e. camera set-ups), giving the director more choices in the edit. More time for the art department to create great sets, and more time for you to rehearse on the floor and get those extra takes if necessary. In some respects, this time you have on a feature can work against you. You may be hanging around for a considerable amount of time after that first rehearsal while they light; and hanging around again between set-ups. You need to conserve your energy and concentration, but make no mistake: on either television or feature you can be working twelve to fourteen hours a day. Rising at 5–5.30 a.m. (for poor actresses with hair and make-up it could be even earlier), travelling to the studio or location, grabbing some breakfast, into costume then make-up and on the set by 8–8.30 a.m., shooting through till 7 p.m. or later, then travelling home, trying your level best to be in bed by 10–10.30 p.m., up again at 5–5.30 a.m., and so on. Now, if you've landed a big fat lead (which is what we're all after), and you're on every day, it can get pretty knackering. A movie can shoot for anything from six weeks to six months. A big television series (an hour each episode) takes from three to six months. *Bleak House* was sixteen half-hours and took around six months, although we did get breaks here and there.

When I worked on *Holby City*, with a budget from £300,000 to £400,000 for a sixty-minute programme, we were shooting eleven to fifteen pages a day, working with two film units, who shot two episodes each, so we were working on four hour-long episodes at the same time, while reading and learning another two episodes which would come into the schedule further down the line. All this meant keeping six different storylines in our heads and learning a huge amount of medical dialogue and chat while carrying out complicated surgical procedures with a proper surgeon at our elbows to make sure each stitch and suture was correct. Oh, and trying to give a performance! I'd never worked under such pressure before, shooting for months at a time at such an intense pace. Ironically, I got a great deal out of it as an actor: I was so plugged into the camera by the time I left, and I now learn faster than ever. Nothing has been as tough as that again.

On a soap like *EastEnders* or *Coronation Street*, you're working with a multi-camera set-up (three to five cameras simultaneously). You could be shooting as much as thirty pages a day (remember the two pages a day on a feature?), and they only allow twenty minutes to record a scene, which can be three to four pages long. You are working with two units, each unit shooting four half-hour episodes at the same time, so you're carrying eight episodes in your head simultaneously.

But then there are another four episodes coming to you that you'll go on to once you've finished a block of four, so you're juggling twelve half-hour episodes in your head at any one time. You're doing that for months... years, possibly. Now that *is* pressure! How these actors function and maintain performances under that schedule, I'll never know. Here's a quote from my friend Jo Joyner, who worked on *EastEnders*:

> We usually have two units running and sometimes three. It's not unusual to be with two units in one day, with very tight crossovers. When you're involved in a heavy storyline you can expect to be in six days a week. The only scenes you may have off would be because you were involved in a make-up change. I'd say that, from an actor's perspective, the best thing about multi-camera is not being left with the feeling that your best take was on your reverse (when you're off camera). You're nearly always covered. I would say that the hardest thing is that it requires even more of a circle of concentration, as there are so many eyes/lenses watching you. You need to be very camera-aware as you've got a lot of other people's shots that you mustn't be blocking.

You can see why getting another take in these circumstances could be difficult, although a very experienced director that I talked to on *EastEnders* said that he'd always try to accommodate an actor in that regard.

Something to bear in mind if you do work at this pace is that when you come onto a production with an easier schedule, you should remind yourself to slow down; that you *can* stop more easily *and* ask for that other take. You'll have trained yourself to work at that breakneck speed, but now you can breathe again and take more time.

# GETTING THE JOB!
## or
# AUDITIONS AND SELF-TAPING

My first piece of advice is: *learn it*. It's no good working to a camera with your face buried in a script; you've got to get your eyes up to that lens.

I met a young actor recently who'd never realised this was the best approach until he saw an actor's screen test, as part of the extras that come with a DVD.

Finally the penny dropped: no one had mentioned in his training that he should learn the scenes, so he would just go in and read. It never occurred to him that learning it was essential... *Hello? Drama schools?*

When you audition, you'll turn up at a casting director's office. There will probably be some other actors who are up for the same role sitting around in some kind of waiting room, even on the stairs in some offices.

There are occasions when you'll be expected to give some kind of performance for a part when you've not even seen a full script, you may just have been sent some pages; this is particularly the case with American productions.

Of course, it's very tough to try and suggest a character that you don't know every detail of, or indeed the context for that character or the narrative or style they're looking for. Sorry to sound a bit negative here, but these are just the facts of life these days. Hopefully your agent will have filled you in as best they can. All you can do is trust your instincts and go for it.

It can also be a bit inhibiting to try and give your best performance in what could be quite a small office, with the casting director's assistant reading in the other lines and operating a rather small digital camera. You may, in fact, only have the casting director there, both operating and reading in, but you should find them sensitive and helpful. They'll fill you in on the character a bit and may well ask you to try it a different way.

I always ask whoever is reading in to step out of my eye-line, then I'll pick an eye-line for myself nice and close to the camera. This is in no way disparaging to anyone, but I'd rather work to a mark than to a non-actor who has their face buried in a script and who may inhibit me when they do decide to make eye contact.

You may well get two or three goes at it, then you'll stagger out into the street and try not to think about the damn job that you want so desperately. Best to have a coffee and forget about it. It'll happen or it won't. You've given it your best shot: the rest is up to them.

I remember the wonderful producer Nigel Stafford-Clark (*Bleak House*) giving advice to some actors in a workshop that I ran. He said: 'Remember, if you're there [for an audition] somebody already rates you, thinks you have talent.' So always take that in there with you, 'I wouldn't be here if somebody didn't rate me.' Let that give you confidence: you deserve to be there.

There is, however, a whole other thing going on with auditions for features and television: SELF-TAPING. A bit of a misnomer since there's no tape any more, just a digital hard drive, but we'll use the taping term nonetheless. If you're busy with something else and can't physically get to a casting it makes perfect sense, at least you get some kind of crack at it. I first became aware of self-taping when I was working on a movie and one of the leading actors was tearing his hair out trying to get something put on camera for a television series he was up for, in the middle of shooting a major role. He got the part, by the way.

The fact is you may well be self-taping at home. You'll have to set up some kind of camera yourself. You'll get the script or pages by email, then record yourself and send it via email to your agent, who'll send it on to the casting department of the production.

There are a couple of alternatives to doing this at home. Some agencies will have their clients come in and go on camera in a spare office. Now this, of course, is good but the feedback I'm getting is that it'll be an agent's assistant reading in, so again you're working with a non-actor and they have a limited amount of time – so there's a sense of arriving there, having little or no time to check how you look, the whole thing feeling a bit rushed, and by the time you've made the journey there, gone on camera and travelled home again, you might better doing it yourself. It would certainly be an advantage if you could take an actor friend with you who you'd rehearsed with, but if you do it on your own, again I'd recommend that you ask the assistant to step out of your eye-line and work to a mark.

Spotlight run a service to facilitate self-taping. They have three studios at their headquarters off Leicester Square in London. They currently charge £65 for an hour, for half an hour it's half that fee. Their studios have a nice professional feel; they're quiet and well appointed. At the time of writing, this service has been running for just over three years, so you can see it's a developing part of the business. Around eighty per cent of the auditions they run are for the States and they're very busy.

I'd certainly recommend taking in a fellow actor if at all possible to read the off-lines. The operators there are very used to reading in, but there's no substitute for the real thing. Make sure your off-camera actor is as close to the lens as possible. You don't need to be sitting, unless it makes sense for the scene you're playing. If it feels better, have the camera raised to eye level or just a hair's breadth above that (it's a better angle for the face). Get things set up to suit *you*: you're the one who's paying!

If I had to do this with the operator reading (as with the casting director), I'd ask them to step out of my eye-line, I'd take in some white gaffer tape so I can attach a small square of it to the lens hood of the camera or on the wall just behind. This would give me a nice clear eye-line to play off, so that if I look away, for a moment, I can come back to that nice steady mark, near the lens. You can have a look at each take after you've done it and make sure you're happy before you move on.

You can have as many as four scenes to get down, which is a lot to learn and to achieve a good result in the time. Plenty of actors are doing this constantly, so it can be quite a pressure, and I guess the cost is an issue.

On the plus side, the image is very good because the camera is of a decent quality, so you'll look reasonable, and there's a proper mic, so the sound is good. They also have pretty fast technology to play back takes and get them downloaded and off to your agent and/or casting directors. There are occasions (particularly from the States), where your test is being watched on Skype, with the director/casting director giving you direction online.

I think it would be a very good idea to build up some experience at home, with whatever you have available, just to practise doing a take then watching it back, trying it a different way, and generally getting used to seeing yourself, so that you become a bit more objective about your own image and don't feel like running screaming from the room at the sight of yourself. You'd then be in a better state to use the Spotlight set-up, or your agent's, to your best advantage.

The advantage you have at home is that you can keep doing it until you have something that you're happy with. This can be time-consuming, it can take hours to get it as you want it – I've heard of instances where there are as many as eighteen pages of dialogue to learn, particularly from the States.

Here's some advice from casting directors I've spoken to:

- Keep it simple in terms of the frame, head and shoulders.

- Not too much effort with suggesting the character, as that can be a distraction; if you're wearing loud earrings, for instance, they can be too interested in those and not you!

- Shoot against a plain wall, with nothing distracting in the back of shot like a picture or things on a mantelpiece.

- Try to get another actor to do the off-lines, and again keep the eye-line close to the lens.

Self-taping is, of course, very useful if you're living outside of London. It can give that first impression: then, if you are asked to meet and spend money on travel, you know that there is at least some interest.

I worked recently with an actress on the television series *New Tricks* who had put herself on camera in Los Angeles and got the role. Generally, though, casting directors like nothing better than having the actor in the room.

# GETTING SET UP

A flip camera can be useful as it plugs straight into a computer, and a tripod is a good idea. In terms of sending the file, you should check with your agent about what's the best file-transfer service to use, which ones will be compatible with their system. Some examples are with a Vimeo account, Hightail or Dropbox.

iPhones are certainly used, and iPads are good since you can edit on them and add your name as a credit before your tape.

I'd suggest setting whatever camera you have at eye level or just a bit above, even if you're standing. If you don't have a tripod and you're using your iPhone, it can best be balanced in a phone dock on top of whatever you can improvise.

Again, it's best if you can have a fellow actor do the off-lines, but I've heard of instances where you record the off-lines on your iPhone in advance, then play that recording while you're taping.

Don't have your back to a window or a light as you'll be 'back-lit' and therefore in silhouette. Put yourself against a blank wall with not too many objects behind you. You can shoot a quick test, then have a look at yourself, make some adjustments to the light, the camera height or yourself, and try again.

Regarding lighting at home, a DOP I worked with, Peter Sinclair, suggests getting a large Chinese-paper lampshade, one of those big white paper balls, with a 100- or 60-watt clear bulb, placing it to one side of you (three feet away or so) as you face the camera.

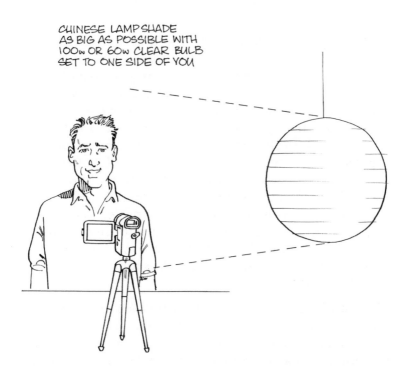

CHINESE LAMPSHADE
AS BIG AS POSSIBLE WITH
100w OR 60w CLEAR BULB
SET TO ONE SIDE OF YOU

Think of self-taping as practice for your film work. I would suggest that you do a few dry runs at this while you're at drama school to get the feel of it. Do a take, and watch each one back, so that by the time you're leaving to go into the profession you're already geared up for those first camera auditions.

I'm going to come clean here: I've never had to do this... *yet*!

Here's some useful information explaining how three actors go about their own self-taping process. English actor Lydia Wilson films her audition on her iPhone, precariously balanced somewhere on hairbrushes or books. She uses a Vimeo account to upload the finished video online. Vimeo can be used for free, but a small monthly subscription allows faster upload times and more storage space. When it's uploaded to Vimeo, Lydia says:

> There's an icon in the right-hand corner of the video screen which is 'Share'. If you click on this, you can enter the email address of your agent, with or without a personal message as you wish, and then you click 'Send'. They'll receive an email saying 'Lydia Wilson has sent you a video' with a link to the video. If you've chosen to add a password (easy to do on Vimeo), then it'll also have the password written in the body of the email. Then your agent can download it and upload it in whatever format they prefer to edit videos, and use their own software to turn it into a link to send to the casting director. I have a very proactive agent so I send her tons of takes, and she edits them.

Vincent Riotta, a bilingual actor who lives in Rome, uses a Canon video camera that cost about £700. He knows some actors who use cheaper cameras, but he also uses his when he teaches film acting in Italy. From the video camera, auditions need to be transferred to a computer and converted into MPEG-4 format using QuickTime or a similar programme. Vincent then uses the online file-sharing website WeTransfer to send files to his agent; they'll make any suggestions about retakes and then pass it on to the casting director. There is definitely an advantage to being able to do as many takes as you want until you get it right. As Vincent says:

> I have gotten a couple of jobs this way, and I hear that many casting directors in the States are accepting self-taping more and more as it widens the net, i.e. English actors doing American accents or for English roles in the States. Even English, French and Italian casting directors are accepting self-taping to find English-speaking actors who aren't necessarily

English, but also to look for mother-tongue English actors.

Magdalena Rodriguez works in the UK, but spends some of her time in Spain. When she started getting auditions and requests to self-tape, she recalls:

Every time I got stressed out trying to find a film-maker friend to help me record the scene and then send online. This was happening for castings taking place in the UK and abroad – sometimes whilst I was in Spain too – so I thought if I invested in a camera I would save time and pressure. I would also make sure that I wouldn't miss any opportunities for work by not having access to the equipment.

Now, she self-tapes on a small flip-video HD camera, which is as light as a mobile phone and the size of a small digital photographic camera. It can easily be placed on any flat surface according to what height is needed, though it's best to use a tripod, in front of a white wall, with no unnecessary distractions. Magdalena does as many takes as she needs, ensuring that the camera's battery stays charged and there's enough storage space on the hard-drive, so that neither run out in the middle of a take.

Recording is, she says, 'like sex: much better shared, but if not, you just work around it.' If you're recording on your own, do a test shoot to make sure you're in the frame, have set up the sort of shot requested (wide shot, close-up, etc.), know your marks, and have got the lighting right.

Recording with somebody else behind the camera makes it easier and more relaxing, as you only need to focus on your job as an actor. The other person can do all the technical stuff and feed you the lines for you to bounce off. They can also give you a more direct eye-line and help with the creative process. But it also depends who it is, as

35

it can be frustrating if they don't know what the heck they are doing (as I said, just like with sex). So getting a fellow actor, or somebody very patient, with experience in film production or photography, is always the best option.

Magdalena downloads all the takes onto her computer, so she can choose the one that she feels shows the best and most natural performance option for the role she's auditioning for:

> If in doubt, I will go through them time and time again, trying to be truthful to the info I've been given in the script and the character breakdown. If possible, I will ask somebody else for their opinion: whether I agree with them or not, it can often help to make up my own mind. I look through as many takes as possible; patience is the key because, as cringe-making as it might be to look at yourself on screen (and analyse your performance, your voice, your body weight, your wrinkles, as we all do), you must try to be objective and put yourself in the shoes of that casting director or whoever is going to see those shots later on, and who will decide if you are what they are looking for.

You need to show yourself at your best, so learn your lines. If you don't have enough time then you can use the script, but as Magdalena warns, 'the important thing is to ensure that the camera sees your eyes during most of the delivery'.

Vincent Riotta almost always memorises his lines, though a couple of times he's put his computer next to the camera and read, trying to hide his darting eyes. Recording the off-lines on a Dictaphone and playing them back wasn't appreciated by his agents. Ideally, you need to get a real actor, not a non-actor or amateur, to act with you. 'You have to believe that the person in front of you is the character in the scene,' he says.

Magdalena always tries to adapt her image in the most simplistic way to the role in question – though wearing a black wig for a tape once didn't go down well with her agent, who said it was ridiculous and distracting. Everything else – losing or gaining weight, hair colour, skin blemishes – can be adapted once you've got the job.

Vincent prefers to meet the director in person; it may be more pressure, but personality enters into the equation more:

> It always feels like a lottery to audition, with or without self-taping, but with self-taping, I feel less in control of my chances of landing the role. There is definitely an advantage to be able to do as many takes as you want until you get it right (at least you don't come out of the taping session feeling 'Shit, I could've done better!'). So with self-taping there is a sense of being master of my own destiny, but then I wonder if they will think the audition was so good just because I must have done twenty takes! All in all, I prefer my chances with a director present, but that may be down to the fact that I'm an experienced actor and know what to expect at an audition.

Magdalena also thinks that self-taping takes some of the pressure off. Then, if you are called to a second round, your nerves don't interfere quite as much, and you can enjoy meeting people and use the excitement in a positive way. She also has an interesting idea about other benefits of taping yourself:

> Self-taping allows you to see the other side of the coin, which is not something we otherwise get to do as actors. By having to record yourself, you are getting a taster of what it's like to be behind the camera. You can also record not only for auditions, but to practise your craft. You can work with a fellow actor to rehearse and shoot a scripted or improvised scene, maybe from

different angles, and learn from the process of the shoot, and then watching the footage on screen. This way you learn what details to avoid when on a film set or in a live casting session, and you get a bit deeper into the actor-camera relationship. The more you practise, the more you get to relax those muscles when working on screen.

Self-taping is now a fact of life, so you need to take a positive attitude towards it, and work out now how you're going to do it. Don't wait until you suddenly need a self-taped audition to complete in a very short time. For now, though, let's assume you get the job and are starting to prepare for it...

# PREPARING FOR THE SHOOT

As I've said, how you approach a script and your character is personal stuff but here's something to consider.

Some years ago I had two big series for the BBC back to back, *Sensitive Skin* and *Bleak House*. I finished *Sensitive Skin*, throwing up in a lay-by on the A1 at midnight on a Saturday (it was in the script), and walked onto the set of *Bleak House* at 8 a.m. on Monday morning.

*Sensitive Skin* was six half-hour episodes, *Bleak House* sixteen half-hours. Eleven hours of scripts in total. I decided to learn both jobs before I started the first. I was learning dialogue in November that I wouldn't shoot till June but as I went through this process, I remembered something that I discovered in theatre: you don't really know what something means until you learn it. So although I'd have to relearn plenty of the material at a later date, I felt I knew what it meant, I'd made decisions about how to say it and therefore why I was saying it. Of course, on the day, on the set, I had to keep fluid and adaptable, but it was a great lesson. I was also reminded of something the late Dirk Bogarde had said many years previously: that he always learned the whole script before he started. Finally I understood why.

Another great advantage of this process is that it's like your own private rehearsal time: the arc of the character begins to fall into place as you develop a deeper understanding of them, because you know and therefore understand the lines.

Of course, learning like this isn't possible on a long-running series or soaps, where scripts are coming at you in rapid succession, but hopefully you'll have the chance when you start out to try this with the first couple of episodes, to help you gain a better understanding of the character, and that will carry you forward into the series. On a long-running series I tend to learn the week ahead over the weekend.

Over the years I've learned to prepare myself for the stage by arriving for that first day of rehearsal having done a lot of work. Knowing chunks of the text, maybe cracking the major speeches, knowing about the play, being really steeped in it, having an opinion about my character, about how they should look, dress, make-up, hair. Only an opinion – in those early stages of rehearsals it's all about constructive discussion with my director, designer and fellow actors.

I've taken that approach to my stage work across to the camera: preparing myself for the shoot, steeping myself in the screenplay. Here, of course, is one of the major differences: little or no rehearsal; maybe with some projects a couple of days, but in a lot of cases none at all, only the readthrough, where you'll have all the heads of department, the writer, the director and producers – there could be as many as another twenty or so onlookers in all. It's easy to feel a bit nervy on these occasions but remember, it's not a performance, no one's judging you. It's got more to do with meeting your fellow actors, the director, and chatting to make-up and costume (if you haven't already met the costume designer, you may set a date to meet).

I've got to a stage now where I'm not that keen on what you might think of as a formal 'rehearsal' in the theatrical sense, and I realised a while ago why. My performance is for the camera and no one else. I don't want to share my performance with anyone. I don't mind an in-depth chat about relationships, maybe read some scenes, but I've come to find rehearsals vaguely embarrassing because my performance is intimate, a very private relationship between me and the lens.

Frankly my favourite form of rehearsal for film is lunch or a drink and a chat with my immediate cast members, I'm quite serious here, to have the chance to get to know one another a bit so that we feel at ease with each other. For my money this is more productive than any amount of structured rehearsal time. I did this for *Bleak House*. I was very busy on another production but managed to arrange and evening drink with the three young actors I would be working with intimately, Anna Maxwell Martin, Carey Mulligan and Patrick Kennedy. This gave us such a head start for the first few days of the shoot.

When I do meet up with the costume and make-up designers, I want to have some ideas about how I'm going to look so that we can have a constructive discussion. Period, of course, is quite specific, but I'm talking about contemporary costume too: what cut of suit do I want? What colour tones? Everything we wear in society says something about us, about our character. Get to know what suits you, what colours you should or shouldn't wear. Make-up? Do you want pale skin tones or something warmer? How about your hair? (Can still make me nervous, this one: there's something about a stranger getting into your hair, quite literally.) If at all possible I'll want to get together with whoever is doing my make-up and hair before the shoot and try some things out, so that I don't hit the make-up chair on my first day at 6.30 a.m., then onto the set by 8 a.m., feeling that I'm not quite happy with how I look: death on a fucking bike, tense, nervous, not ready for the lens.

With costume, if it's contemporary you'll quite often be taken shopping with the designer: keep your wits about you; concentrate. Keep your eyes open, and work. Don't just wander along being presented with this and that, find things yourself, make a contribution; I guess I'm talking to the men here more: it matters what you wear! And make sure you have a full-length mirror. I've learned to look at a costume very, very hard and ask myself this question: *What's wrong with it?* If there's nothing wrong with it, then we must be on the right track.

This took a lot of learning and still takes a lot of concentration, so don't be swayed by, 'Oh that looks great!' from the designer or anyone else. Keep your cool, keep your counsel, keep quiet, until you know whether it's right or wrong; that you're comfortable. Again, I want to emphasise that all of the above is conducted in the spirit of constructive discussion; it's a collaboration. That's perhaps one of the crucial differences between the stage and the camera; it's a more intensely collaborative process with an entire unit, as opposed to the more direct dynamic of the theatre, between the director, the actors and the audience.

# USING YOURSELF

There's an analogy that the musician uses an instrument but that we actors are our own instrument. Let me take that a little bit further. The most potent weapon we have at our disposal as actors is ourselves. Each one of us is completely unique. As a drama student I was convinced that I was intrinsically uninteresting as a person. I was from a small, provincial Scottish town; I'd been abroad only once; ostensibly, I had a happy, lower-middle-class, rural upbringing. I had nothing to say for myself. So in order to be 'interesting' as a performer, I had to, well... 'perform'. I had to *be* someone else, in order to hold my audience. I remember around that time reading comments by two great actors, John Gielgud and Ralph Richardson (sirs both). They both said roughly the same thing: 'It takes thirteen or fourteen years to become a useful actor.' What the fuck did that mean? Thirteen or fourteen years? Now, obviously, by that point in time you've had plenty of experience and developed a strong technique, but, as I look back on it now, it seems quite clear. The majority of actors start in the profession at around twenty to twenty-one years old; so thirteen to fourteen years of work brings you up to your mid-thirties. And it's around this time, as a person, that you stop apologising for who you are: you begin to feel self-confident – a confidence in yourself that you are, in fact, interesting, that you might have something to say, that you can bring an element to your work that can be really scary... *you*.

It happened to me in long runs in the West End, in two different musicals, *Pal Joey* and *Mr Cinders*. I guess it had something to do with the constant repetition, the feeling of being completely at home on the stage. I began to realise that the bits of myself that I exposed to the audience felt very powerful; there was a connection, an honesty about that. It was around this time that I got my first major movie role, *Local Hero*. That feeling of 'centring' the performance, letting it come out of *me*, became very clear and strong. Until then I'd invariably subverted my natural Scottish roots, used any accent apart from my own, but from that point on, unless the character absolutely demands it, I bring *me* to the table.

Of course, it's part of an actor's equipment to be able to transform ourselves from part to part. Changing our appearance, altering our movement, our body language. But what can be equally challenging is *nothing*: just to be *you*. To have the confidence to work in front of an audience or in front of a camera and not *do* but *be*: peel back the layers to reveal yourself, and, through the sheer force of your concentration, to take the audience on a journey while appearing to be doing nothing, to be still, to be just you. That takes nerve and confidence. The camera certainly loves it, but take that ability back on to the stage and it can be very powerful. I certainly feel now that if I'm straining and pushing for something, it's wrong.

In fact, when I'm playing a leading role on film, when I'm the central, pivotal character and the audience are seeing the story through my eyes, I feel I'm leading them through it, and I don't want to get in their way. Again, huge concentration and an absolute knowledge of the subtext are required, but the performance should be uninflected, not too much in their face. I'm reminded of a movie called *Three Days of the Condor*, a wonderful political thriller, in which Robert Redford's central performance demonstrates this point of view perfectly. For me he's always had a wonderful concentration and focus to his work. For a more contemporary example, have a look at his performance in *All is Lost*, a masterclass in economy. It's made all the more interesting by the almost complete lack of dialogue.

In the recent BBC drama *Legacy*, the young, leading actor, Charlie Cox, gives a similarly concentrated, still performance. These kind of performances make the audience work themselves and invest in the emotional journey you're taking them on.

The late Leonard Bernstein had a wonderful television series, many years ago, called *Young People's Concerts*, where he played and discussed music. He said: 'Never get in the way of the music and the audience.' This describes perfectly what I'm trying to express.

When Billy Wilder first directed Jack Lemmon (a wonderful stage actor), there was a particular take that Wilder had Lemmon do over and over again. 'Too much,' Wilder would say, 'Do it again.' Finally, Wilder said, 'That's it.' Lemmon replied, 'But I'm not doing anything!' 'Exactly,' said Wilder.

# LACK OF PERFORMANCE

You're on a set with say thirty technicians and a few other actors. Now you can be as amusing as you like with the crew and your fellows, but when it comes to the take and the camera is rolling, you are only there for the camera, you are not there to give a 'performance' for the director, the crew or indeed the other actors. You are only there to affect the camera; maybe no one on the set but the soundman (and anyone else with a pair of cans on) can hear you; you may well be so minimal with your face that nothing appears to be happening. This is all as it should be. All that matters at the end of the day is your relationship with the lens and the film/hard drive that's running through the guts of the camera. That's where your performance is going; that is your crucial relationship. Everyone else (even sometimes your fellow actors) is secondary to that. Sacrilege,

I know, to us generous, supportive British actors, but that's how far I've come away from my stage roots.

# LACK OF PROJECTION

I talked earlier about flattening delivery, not being too 'emphatic' with the lines, not pressing on them. This issue is a little tricky to illustrate in a book but the fact is you *can* talk more quietly on a film set than you would in life. If I'm asked to lift the volume up a bit before a take by the sound recordist, firstly I won't be too pleased, but secondly, when I do (and I often forget to), it will be an infinitesimal rise. I will not suddenly start projecting: we're dealing with highly sophisticated recording equipment, so all we need to do is squeeze it up a fraction.

At the top end of the scale you can be as loud as you like; if you need to get emotional and scream the place down, absolutely go for it! I quite often find that I'll strain my voice while filming in a way that I wouldn't do in theatre, because I'm not supporting my voice with my abdomen as I would on stage. I don't want it to be technical; I want it as truthful as I can make it.

There *are* characters that are louder than others. I have found that from time to time I'll be doing early scenes with a character and think, 'My God, I'm being a bit loud here,' but it's just a response to that particular role and I'll go with it. You don't need to be dead quiet and mumble every role on camera, but it's terrific when you begin to realise how quiet you can be, and jump off from that level to be very emphatic indeed. Have a look at Al Pacino in *Glengarry Glen Ross* and *Heat*. You'll see him play around with very low key then very high delivery, verging on the theatrical.

# GETTING UP EARLIER

In the theatre your body clock is geared to the evening: acting is much more of a night-time occupation. Even in rehearsals you're starting at around 10–10.30 a.m., gradually moving into the day's work as you warm up emotionally and physically. But shooting can be a severe shock to the system. You're up at 5–5.30 a.m. and on the set by 8 a.m., trying to... *act*! It's just not natural! Part of my preparation is to begin to rise earlier over a week or so before the shoot, so that by the time I'm on the eve of shooting, I've been rising half an hour or so before my pick-up time (say 5.15–6 a.m.) for the past three to four days. I've gradually adjusted my body clock to filming hours. This is all part of the process of helping that first day feel more like your second or third.

When I started out, I'd feel, during those first few days on the set, very disorientated and almost nauseous with fatigue, almost like jet lag, and that's no way to work. Many years ago I was having dinner with some friends and Frederic Forrest, a vastly experienced American movie actor, and I discovered that he did exactly the same thing. I know it's not an earth-shattering piece of advice, but it all helps, believe me.

# COSTUME

There are occasions when I'm keen to get into costume early. When I meet the costume designer before the shoot, to try on clothes or go shopping, I may well ask if they can get costumes over to my house before the shoot, so that I can wear them in a bit. I don't want to feel that I'm wearing a 'costume'. I don't want the clothes to wear me; I want to wear the clothes. I don't want to be thinking about the clothes at all when I wander in front of the camera. Shoes are crucial: there's something about your feet as an actor. I think it was Olivier who talked about working from the feet up. If it's contemporary, I can wear the clothes out of the house, get used to them, get them into my body shape, so on that first day in front of the camera, they don't feel at all strange or new, they feel like mine.

Period costume is, of course, a different ball game: you can't nick down to Tescos in a Restoration wig and heels (well, maybe *you* can), but you can wear them at home.

In the comedy series *Bob Martin* I had a very camp, contemporary character to play, flamboyant in the extreme, with a matching dress sense. I wanted to work on a particular body language for him, so I got some of the costumes delivered to my home and, whenever I worked on the lines, I wore one of them. I 'rehearsed' on my own, walking, moving, imagining the other characters, getting the right walk, getting my feet right, arms, sinking myself into a different body language.

I played a violent psychotic in a one-off drama for the BBC called *One Way Out*, and I wore cowboy boots, battered jeans, a leather jacket and an old Italian Borsalino (Stetson); I grew a beard and my hair, and had my ear pierced. I wore the costume, out and about, over a week or so, feeling 'invincible' and a bit dangerous. Then I took that attitude out in front of the camera.

# THE ARC OF A PRODUCTION

It's important that you realise that the shooting of a movie/television drama, is only part of an overall process. Essentially there are three distinct periods in any production:

47

- Pre-production (or **prep**)
- The **shoot**
- Post-production (or **post**)

Pretty well every production you see, be it movie, one-off television drama, four-parter, long-running soap or sitcom, will start life as a treatment. This is generally a two- or three-page document which outlines the basic storyline and principal characters: it's a selling document, put together by a writer in order to gain a commission to write the full script. In other words he/she wants to be paid while he/she writes, a perfectly reasonable expectation. It takes great skill and experience to create a readable, exciting, condensed version of what will eventually be anything from a feature film to a major television series lasting several hours or, indeed, several years. It's very possible that the project has been initiated by a producer, who then brings a writer on board to put the treatment together.

For our purposes I'm going to take a movie as a working model (believe me, there's nothing simple or straightforward in this mad business we're all involved in, but the evolution of a movie is ironically more suitable to our purpose than the complex jungle of modern television). Do bear in mind that this is a 'model' and that there are dozens of permutations of this process.

Okay, so here we go: a writer has a brilliant idea for a feature film, he writes a treatment, he submits it to one or more film production companies for consideration and, eventually, one of them bites. It's a strong idea, perhaps there's a connection (the writer is experienced or might have worked with this particular producer before), the producer likes it, he commissions the writer to write a full script. Some kind of deadline will be set, maybe six months. Our beloved writer goes away, sweats, screams, cries, does the washing up, anything to avoid actually writing, and, what do you know, only a month late, delivers a hundred pages of fabulous typing, dialogue, stage directions, etc.... and waits.

You'll remember the general rule of thumb that each page of a screenplay runs at about a minute of screen time (this also applies to television). The ideal length for a movie script is around ninety minutes (so approximately ninety pages). This is because it can then be shown four times a day at the cinema, therefore increasing the chances of making a profit. Make no mistake, when you enter the realms of television or the movie business that is exactly what you are becoming involved in: a business, or 'the industry', as it's often referred to. It's profit and loss: it's how much did you make on the first weekend? It's viewing figures; it's how much washing powder or car insurance they can sell in the ad breaks. And we have to keep our cool and do the best job we can.

The producer comes back to the writer with a bunch of notes. 'It's too long, it's too slow; the central character isn't likable enough and should be a woman not a man (What's-her-face would be great!); don't like the ending, it's too downbeat,' etc., etc.... There'll be a meeting, face to face, a discussion (let's hope an amicable one), the writer goes away, screams, cries, washes up, rewrites, and some weeks later delivers (note this term) the second draft of the screenplay. He waits... More notes, more discussion, he wants to keep the central character as a man and can't stand What's-her-face anyway. This process continues over some months. Let's say, for the sake of argument, the writer's script is finally acceptable to the producer after twenty drafts.

All right, the producer now takes their baby out into the big cold world of film finance. He's hoping to raise, say, six million pounds; he doesn't have six million pounds of his own, and even if he had he wouldn't be dumb enough to risk his own money. Six million is not a low budget by British standards: that would be somewhere between one and two million pounds (I recently worked on a wonderful British sci-fi movie, *The Machine*, with a budget of only £750,000). Six million is a relatively comfortable budget, that would allow them a reasonable time, say ten to twelve weeks, to shoot the movie. It's a very complex business, putting finance together for a feature; it's often done on an international scale, patched together possibly through Europe and America, and it can take a long... long time.

It's often essential to have an actor or two attached to the project (here's the tough 'industry' bit) – actors who are 'bankable', whose name will attract investment and sell the product. Yes, I said product. There are no rules here, but from inception, it can easily take five years to get a movie set up and shot. I think the script for the movie *Unforgiven* was around for about fifteen years before Clint Eastwood picked it up and got it made. One producer told me recently that they had been working with a writer on a script for one and a half years and had spent, up to that point, a million pounds, and had still not gone into production.

So let's assume all the money's there and doesn't suddenly disappear at the last minute (quite common, let me assure you). Now come some comments from the money men/producers. They're putting up the finance so they have a right to their say (our poor, benighted writer, by this time, is in therapy or rehab). More meetings, more discussions and up come another few drafts, let's say another three: that puts us at twenty-three so far, but now the director comes on board and has some suggestions for changes to the script, another couple of drafts ensue, where are we now: twenty-five. This is extremely modest by the way; it could be well over a hundred.

Right – *finally* – a schedule is drawn up for prep, the shoot and post.

# PRE-PRODUCTION (PREP)

Depending on the scale of the movie (in other words, the budget), the pre-production period can be anywhere from three to six months, or longer.

First, a line producer will be brought in to manage the production, to deal at first hand with the management of the budget on a day-to-day basis.

Then various heads of department or HODs are brought on board at anything from four to twelve weeks prior to the shoot, and often more on big features. These will include:

- The art director: who will design sets, dress and adapt various locations on the production. Lots of discussions here with the director about the look and colour tones for the film. He/she will have a team of assistants working under them.

- The costume designer: again a lot of discussion with the director and the art director.

- The 1st assistant director, location manager and production manager: who come on board closer to the shoot, say four weeks before.

- Around two weeks before, comes the director of photography or DOP, a crucially important figure for us – oh brother, are they ever! He/she will work very closely with the director: this is one of the most important relationships on the unit, because they will have such an impact on the atmosphere, the light and shade (quite literally), the movement of the camera and the style of the final piece.

- The head of make-up: also comes in around two weeks before.

- The sound department: later still (first day of the shoot).

- The editor won't come on board until the shoot begins.

All of these departments will have, by their input, a huge impact on the final product that emerges in what could be a year of intense work. I'm talking, of course, about the length of the whole production, not just the shoot.

# THE SHOOT

But wait! What's this I see approaching? – *oh no!* It's *a covey!* A bunch! A herd of – Christ! Oh Jesus no! Run for the fucking hills! Here come *the actors*!!

Here's the crux of what I've been driving at: we come in and do our job, lifting the script from the page and breathing life into it (quite literally), perhaps taking it in directions that neither the writer, producer nor the director expected, hopefully surprising them, in a good way, releasing elements that no one else had spotted were lurking there. But by the very nature of the beast – the machine we're working in – we have to be pliable and adaptable, able to play off the top of our heads, turn on a dime, play it an entirely different way, all on the basis of only a rehearsal on the floor, on the day, possibly with actors we have never met ('Yes, this is Ethel, now if you'd like to get your clothes off and jump into bed, we'll get started'). We need to be thoroughly prepared but totally spontaneous, able to fly by the seat of our pants, immediately they shout: 'Turn over!' And to deal with changes to the script, possibly on a daily basis. It was Francis Ford Coppola who said, 'A script is like a newspaper, it changes every day.'

It's very important to realise that, at the end of our job, when we walk away convinced we'll never work again, the next process is already beginning...

# POST-PRODUCTION (POST)

The editor and the director begin the editing process, creating the tempo and style of the piece. If I had my way, every drama student/aspiring actor would spend time in an editing suite. You learn more about film acting there than anywhere because you can begin to piece together the concept that you are giving the camera, and therefore the editor and director, 'options' to play with in the edit. You'll begin to understand what not to waste your valuable energy on and where the 'meat' of your performance lies, in terms of shots. In the edit, your very intention within a scene can be changed by the simple turn of a head, either cut or added. Believe me, the possibilities are endless.

When the edit is finished, you have the dub, where sound is added – background noise, traffic, birds, whatever – building, with the music (and how potent a force is that!), an aural backdrop to the visual experience which makes the movie. We actors may well be brought back here to do ADR (explanation to follow).

Then comes the grade. With modern technology, the colour, even the light and shade within the scenes, can be radically altered with just the push of a button or the click of a mouse. The grader or the colourist (in conjunction with the DOP) can, for instance, bring out all the blues in a particular scene, change the colour of specific objects in a scene. It's frankly staggering how you can change the image: creating, in a sense, the final draft of the finished film. The producers will certainly be keeping an eye on the edit, making suggestions. They and the director may want to pick up shots they feel are missing (pick-ups). This means we may have to come back, months after we've wrapped, to do close-ups or scenes for a character that we've totally obliterated from our memory banks, possibly without our fellow actors there. (We'll discuss this later.)

If you're ever in a position to see the rough cut of a film you're in, be aware you're *not* watching the final product. The picture will be ungraded (so you will not look your best), the sound will not be balanced properly, the final music may well not be on, and there will still be fine-tuning to be done on the edit. The result of all this is that you may well stagger out of that screening thinking you're shite, that you've screwed up your performance and that your career is over! Rough cuts are hard to watch and hard to judge, so be realistic about what you're seeing – or avoid them.

Here's a wonderful quote from the late, great director Sidney Lumet (*Dog Day Afternoon, Serpico, Running On Empty*) on the film-making process:

> In a sense a movie is constantly being rewritten. The various contributions of the director and the actors, the music, sound, camera, decor and editing, are so powerful that the movie is always changing. All these factors add digressions, increase or subtract from clarity, change the mood, or tip the balance of the story. It's like watching a column of water whose colour keeps changing as different dyes are added. In movies it's inevitable, and as long as the primary intention has been kept, the new elements should be welcome. All of the individual contributions add up to a total far greater than their individual parts. Movie-making is very much like an orchestra: the addition of various harmonies can change, enlarge and clarify the nature of the theme.

# WHO DO I WANT TO MEET?

It's my first day shooting. When I walk onto a set for the first time, I will be taken on by one of the 3rd assistant directors (3rd ADs).

The 2nd AD liaises directly with the actors, dealing with your call times, transport, etc., and is rarely on set.

The 3rd AD is on set most of the time, dealing with dozens of different tasks, working under the 1st AD and/or the 2nd AD (off-set).

As I walk onto the set I'll ask them to introduce me to the 1st assistant director or that will be done automatically. Now the 1st AD is a very powerful figure on the unit: he/she runs the set for the director, they will have worked closely with the director and the DOP on the preparation (prep) for the entire shoot. They will have worked their way up from 3rd AD, to 2nd then 1st. It's a bloody hard job: they never let up all day, often discussing things with the director over lunch, keeping the set moving, keeping the director up to schedule. The 1st is the liaison between the director, the actors and the crew: they can and should be a really useful ally for you while you're working.

I'll already have met the director (that is how I got the job in the first place), naturally I'll greet him/her in a professional and cordial manor, but he/she is not who I'm really interested in at this stage. I'll then ask the 1st AD to introduce me to the person with whom I will have the most intimate of relationships on the set: the operator. This is the person who will actually record my performance, who will scrutinise it through the camera itself, who (with the help of the camera crew) will stick to me like a limpet, whether I'm doing an intense, very still close-up or running full tilt for several hundred yards down a street. This is a relationship I will cultivate.

The 2nd AD will get in touch to give me my first call time (when I'm due at the location) and my pick-up time (normally you'll be picked up by car and driven to work, although on some long-running series/soaps, you have to make your own way). They'll give you a call sheet at the end of each day. Call sheets give the whole unit a breakdown of the next day's work, i.e. when you'll be required and what scenes are to be shot.

Before my first day's shooting, I'll ask the 2nd AD to get a unit list to me. This is all very standard stuff, by the way. A unit list will run to maybe half a dozen pages and will list all the personnel on the film unit apart from the actors. It will tell me the names in the make-up and wardrobe departments, for instance, who I'll be dealing with closely on a daily basis, but I'm searching for four or five names most particularly:

- the director of photography (DOP)
- the camera operator
- the focus puller (or 1st assistant cameraman/ 1st AC)
- the clapper loader (or 2nd assistant cameraman/ 2nd AC)
- And the grip

Before I get to that first day, I'll try and memorise everyone's names.

The director of photography is responsible for lighting scenes for the camera. After the director, he/she is the most powerful person on the set. *Good lighting is everything!* It is, of course, incredibly important on the stage, but it's paramount on camera. Some years ago I was involved in two series, both six-parters. The lighting on the first series was superb and really quite poor on the second. This affected the atmosphere of the piece very badly, and I'm convinced it contributed to the fact that the series was not recommissioned.

I'll break down the rest of the camera crew for you. The DOP will have his/her choice of operator (although the producer and the director may have an influence here). As the name implies, the operator operates the camera during takes. They're 'on' all day (and fourteen-hour days are quite common), their concentration and commitment is extraordinary. I've certainly had occasion to quietly ask an operator what he/she thought of a take I'd just done. These days, sadly, the director will watch the take on a separate monitor, wearing headphones, possibly in another room. For my money, the best place for a director during a take (unless there's too much camera movement) is standing or sitting by the camera itself, but these days that's almost unheard of. There seems to be an obsession now with making sure that the shots are framed properly, which is, of course, the operator's job and he/she should be trusted to do it. My feeling therefore is that it's the operator who is viewing my performance as intensely as anyone else. There are occasions when the DOP will operate as well – usually to save money on the budget – and there are some DOPs who actually prefer to operate themselves.

During a take, the focus puller (1st AC) will be adjusting the focus of the lens to make sure that your image stays sharp, that you don't go 'soft' or out of focus. While you're rehearsing the scene with the camera, the focus puller will be measuring the distance from the camera to the actor's faces so that they know what focal length the shot has to be and how it might vary during the take. That's why you invariably have marks to hit so that you work in concert with the camera, keeping your image sharp and in the right position within the frame of the shot. The focus puller is probably the hardest technical job on set. Film cameras have a lot more electronics in them now and he/she must also have an in-depth knowledge of the various HD cameras that are becoming more and more common in film-making. When you're shooting with film proper, the focus puller will load the film into the camera itself, threading the film in and around the various cogs that pull the film over the shutter of the camera to expose it. They will almost certainly go on to operate and then possibly progress to DOP.

The clapper loader (2nd AC) will assist the whole camera crew, put the clapperboard in before each take and fill in sheets that keep a record for the editor of all the shots that are taken. On an HD camera there is no 'loading' of film to do: it's either a disc, or the image goes straight onto the hard drive in the camera itself.

A reel of film on a 35mm camera lasts for eleven minutes and six seconds, and on a 16mm camera it's ten minutes and forty seconds, so the clapper loader has to keep track of precisely how many feet of film are left in any reel. It's a real crime if the film runs out in the middle of a take; thankfully it's rare, but bloody irritating if it does happen. On HD cameras the trend is now to have cameras with no moving parts, disc or tape. Most now record on hard drives, or memory cards, and these can vary from twenty, forty or sixty minutes, depending on the quality of the image required, i.e. the higher the quality of the image, the more memory it uses, so the shorter the time.

Next is the grip. Whenever the camera needs to be shifted from one set-up (camera position) to another, or moved during a take, it's the grip who does it. The camera is usually mounted on a dolly: this is a seriously heavy piece of equipment, which is moved on rubber wheels. It can take the camera on a motorised mount that can be raised or lowered to whatever height is required, during takes if necessary. The DOP can sit on it, and it has the capacity to take the director on board as well: so you can see that it's a very substantial piece of equipment. I discovered only recently that the dolly was first developed for loading bombs into planes.

If you're shooting interior scenes and the floor is very level, then the grip can move the camera fairly easily directly on the floor, as long as it's completely silent (no creaky floorboards), but invariably a track will be laid, certainly if you're shooting exteriors. Tracks are best described as mini, tubular, steel railway lines; they come in varying lengths and are slotted together to give whatever length of track is required. The grip is in charge of laying the tracks with the help of a chippy (carpenter), a stagehand and a construction rigger.

There are occasions when you'll be required to cross tracks during a take, even to walk along them, without appearing to do so. This can be a bit tricky, but the thing to do is get your feet used to the moves they have to make to accommodate the tracks; just rehearse it a few times for yourself, while the crew are busy setting up other things. So the grip is there behind the camera during the takes. They'll have the script of the scene attached to the camera, and be watching the actors like a hawk with a small monitor mounted on the dolly as back-up. They'll be squeezing the camera along at exactly the right tempo and hitting their own marks, which match the shot size and focus of each shot, in conjunction with the dialogue, working as a member of a seamless ensemble with the rest of the camera crew and the actors. There are plenty of occasions when the grip will be moving the camera at great speed, even backwards sometimes!

I'll often ask the grip if the speed of my movement is matching theirs with the camera, can they cope with it if I go a bit faster, for instance? The answer is usually yes. But there are occasions where you do have to accommodate the grip. If you're sitting down or stand-ing up, you may well have to slow those movements down so that the grip, and therefore the operator, can keep you in the frame. It's also very possible that if you're in a mid-shot or a close-up and you're running, you'll need to slow the run down for the same reasons.

This can feel a bit unnatural but it will look fine in the shot. So I'm working closely with the grip, making the shots work with them and the rest of the camera crew.

Now, of course, sound is incredibly important; if you can't be heard well, that ain't so good. The sound department breaks down fairly simply. On average there are three personnel: the sound mixer, who's the head of sound and who actually runs the recording machine (like most other technology, this has become digital), and another one or two people who'll be on boom mics. A boom is a long, sausage-shaped microphone, attached to a long pole so that it can be dangled (as it were) just above your head or held just below you, to record your dialogue. On exteriors they add a casing round the mic and a furry covering, this is to cut down exterior sound, like wind.

Because the boom operators want to get the microphone as close to you as possible, it can happen that the boom comes into the shot itself: this might stop a take immediately, and it's quite common. The boom can also create shadows on the set if it catches the light: this can also stop a take, or may mean going again on a take. You'll hear the operator say, 'Boom shadow.' The alternative is to use throat mics: these are the very small mics that you'll see often on television, in news interviews, attached to a person's jacket or blouse. For our purposes they are hidden in a tie or under a T-shirt – as close to your mouth as they can comfortably get. Sound mixers prefer the quality of sound on the boom mics, which is why they are used whenever possible.

For an actress, the small mic can be tricky: if she's wearing a dress it may be tucked into the cleavage. Then there's a little battery pack that needs to be secreted somewhere. For men it can be simply tucked into a jacket pocket, the back pocket of trousers or a belt, for women it can mean strapping it to the inside of the thigh or the small of the back under the costume. Once it's in place I'm usually happier with a throat mic: you soon forget about it, and there's no danger of that 'boom in shot' scenario.

The sound mixer's trolley, with boom mics.

It's crucial for me that I feel at home with the crew members that I'm facing during a take (they're almost always very nice people, by the way). In a very real sense I want to be one of them, to be working in concert with them, both while we're rehearsing and, of course, during the actual takes. So on that first day that I walk on the set I say hello to them, shaking hands, asking them how it's going, and generally making friends.

Actors are normally referred to as 'artists' on the set, a term I find a bit pretentious, frankly – I'd rather be called 'The Acting Department', because that's how I like to think of myself, as another department, part of the unit. It's part of the pleasure of the job, this collaboration with these dedicated professionals.

# THE SHOOTING PROCESS

If your director knows what they're doing, they will clear the set entirely when you rehearse for the first time. At a stretch, the DOP might squeeze into a corner, and the script supervisor, who can keep an eye on the lines – but, remember, don't expect her to prompt you, these are not theatrical people (though if you ask her to do so, she will). You'll find that a lot of experienced actors will still have their scripts – or their sides – in their hands at this stage.

Let me talk about sides. When you stagger into your trailer at some ungodly hour in the morning, you'll find a much smaller version of the call sheet (a quarter size), which will include the scenes to be shot that day. These are called sides, and the majority of actors will walk onto the set to rehearse with sides in their determined mitts rather than a full-size script. They're easier to carry while you rehearse; you can stuff them into a pocket or whatever; they are very convenient... and I don't like them. When I'm on the set, I want to have my full script beside me at all times, because ten to one during rehearsals, or just as we're running up to a take, I'll want to check where exactly this scene comes in the narrative. When did the audience last see me? How long is it since they've seen me? (A minute a page, remember?) If we're doing a series, it could have been a week since they had certain information. What was my emotional state like in the previous scenes? Where is my character going after this scene? A dozen different questions that can't be answered by sides. It's very easy to get separated from your script on a set, but I try to keep mine within arm's reach at all times – even during takes it'll be on the floor by my feet or just out of shot. If, by chance, you do lose sight of it, there is one person on the set who can help you: the script supervisor. Among her many functions, it's her job to keep track of the narrative of the story, principally for the director, but she will be able to supply the answers to some of the questions above, pretty quickly. Now, of course, I've prepared myself for the shoot, knowing my lines and building up a sense of the narrative, but in the heat of the set, fighting a tough schedule, it's invaluable to have that full script there.

Another reason I like my script with me is that it's *mine*: I've worked with it in my preparation, made notes in it, made dialogue changes, scrubbed out stage directions: it's nice and messy and it belongs to me. The sides are clean, unsullied and belong to the production. It's part of my process to take control of the script as I take control of the character and the performance.

There is no upstage or downstage on film. When you're rehearsing with the director on the set for the first time, remember you're playing in the round. The nearest stage equivalent, in terms of style, to working on camera is playing in a small studio theatre in the round. Don't be drawn towards the director in the rehearsal, don't play towards him/her; use the set as though there is no one else there. Your back may be towards him/her for the entire scene or you may elect to play the entire scene staring out of a window. It's a good idea to get onto a set before you rehearse, if possible, to get a feel of it, see what the geography is, what might be interesting to use. It may be a set that's particularly relevant to your character, so try and feel comfortable in it, sit in the chairs, try the desk, pick up the phone, whatever.

Hopefully you'll run the lines for the scene before you start, and it's quite common to have the script in your hand if you need it (this is entirely personal). It's at this stage that you can bring up any problems with the dialogue; if a line just doesn't make sense to you or it feels extraneous, you may want to cut it. I may well have a suggestion for a new line or two, or transpose lines to help rhythm and sense.

I've already talked about possible lack of accuracy in dialogue when filming (as opposed to the stage), that I'm more interested in character and the emotional journey. In fact, I'm very prone to rewriting dialogue, coming up with alternative 'end lines' for scenes, cutting dialogue that I find extraneous or repetitive. I will often want to simplify lines so that they are easier to say – I don't want to be 'working too hard' to wrap my tongue around some awkward bit of syntax unless it's entirely necessary. Of course, this is after many years of experience and may be a difficult approach for you to take when you're starting out.

This situation varies from job to job, but if you have to justify those cuts and rewrites it should be done in a constructive and collaborative way. What I still find hard to get used to (I'm talking about television here) is that these discussions are often had with the producer rather than the director. This isn't always the case, but it's more and more common now, and I still find it a bit odd. I guess it's because I come from a theatrical background where I expect the director to have complete autonomy and control, but this is how contemporary television functions now.

Okay, so you block the scene. It's got a reasonable shape, though you may well still be finding moments that aren't quite working for you. If so, that's fine: don't panic. Think of it as 'cooking up' into the take; you don't necessarily want to give your full emotional commitment to the scene till that camera rolls. Now the DOP (if he hasn't squeezed himself into a corner for the rehearsal) will come in to have a look at what you've got, and the director and the DOP will then decide what the shots are going to be, i.e. how they'll cover the scene. The DOP may suggest some slightly different positions for the actors for technical reasons: the position of the camera, what's in the background, or the direction of light. For instance, you may be shooting against a window, so you're dealing with daylight, which is changeable and which may make it impossible for you to be in a particular position. To reiterate: I don't really care where I'm standing on a film set. All I'm interested in is the shot. Is the shot good? Are we all (the actors/director/operator and DOP) creating interesting frames together? Adjustments are made then the HODs come in: that'll be the full camera crew, the sound department, costume and make-up, props and sparks (electricians). You'll run the scene for them, so that they can see what it entails from their perspective. You suddenly find you have a small audience, but don't be tempted to 'perform' unless it suits you, unless you want to try something out – you're only there for the camera, remember. After this run, marks will start to go down; the camera assistant will be at your feet sticking various colours of gaffer tape on the floor (a different colour for each actor). These marks are not necessarily final, they can still be adjusted. You'll work the scene with the operator, fine-tuning positions; if tracks are required, for instance, they'll be laid.

At this point the actors are released to go back to their trailers, have make-up checks and/or generally arse around. On television, against a tight schedule, this break could be pretty short (fifteen to twenty minutes); on a feature (depending on the budget) it could literally be hours! Be careful of this period, it's very easy to get distracted; buggering around with your other actors, trying to pull the head of make-up, whatever. You've got the scene to shoot. Keep your concentration, keep working the scene for yourself, or run the lines with the other actors if they're agreeable. Apart from that you're probably better on your own, in your trailer, however modest, saving your energy and focus for the camera.

Right: the set's been lit, and we're called back on, usually by the 3rd AD or a runner. There could easily be a couple of 3rd ADs and a runner on a television unit, many more on a big feature. Runners are more like beginners, who work their way up to 3rds, getting a toehold in the industry – and believe me, they *run*! All bloody day! They even have lunch on the run. If you need some water before a take and there's a 3rd or a runner in sight, they'll get it for you. If they're not around, mention it to the 1st AD and he/she'll get it on the set for you pronto. If you need a pee and you need to step off the set, tell a 3rd, a runner or the 1st where you're going. These are small details, I know, but it's no good going into a take with a dry throat or a full bladder; both conditions can get in the way of your concentration. If you're playing a leading or a major supporting role, it's very common that a 3rd or a runner will get your breakfast when you arrive and your lunch; this saves you the time and effort of queueing with the entire unit at the catering truck.

You begin to rehearse with the camera again. The initial marks may well be changed and new ones added. There could also be lighting adjustments going on. You will have the focus puller measuring the distance from the camera to you, usually to your eye so that you're clear and in focus. They quite often use a red laser beam now rather than a tape measure. They may well also put down marks, in white gaffer, which are only for the focus puller's reference: you ignore them. It's very possible that in some shots you'll be 'soft' in the frame. For instance, you might be in the foreground of the shot with another actor in the background, and at some point in the take the focus puller will pull focus onto the other actor so that your image becomes blurred or soft; then the focus may shift back to you at some point, and the other actor becomes soft in the frame. If you watch any television or movie, you'll spot this quite easily.

# COVERAGE

Before we actually begin to shoot it, I'll want to know the sequence of the shots for the scene: what is the coverage for the scene? There are an infinite number of ways to shoot any scene. A standard way would be a wide shot first, then mid-shots (cut off the waist), then close-ups, but that's just one scenario. The reason I want to know the sequence of the shots is so that I can pace myself through the shooting of the scene. It's possible that the director wants to shoot the scene in one shot and that's it. If that's the case, I might be expecting close-ups (which I often think of as the 'meat' of my performance, when I really want to be on the boil), only to discover that there aren't any. So I've been working my way towards my close-ups when I've only got the wide shot. It's also possible that the coverage is really quite extensive and complex and that it's obvious that this scene is going to take quite some time to get in the can. It could easily be hours before we get from that first wide shot to my close-ups, and I need to be aware of that so that I can conserve my energy and concentration.

Obviously, the director knows the sequence of these shots, having worked it out with the DOP after watching our initial rehearsal. In fact, as they discuss the shots, I'm listening carefully to their conversation, beginning to build up a sense of the sequence they're after. This won't necessarily tell me everything I need to know, and things may change, but any clarification

I need I can get from the 1st; it's part the 1st's job to know exactly what the shots are going to be, in what order and size. There are occasions (if we have an easy relationship) when I'll ask the director, but they may have enough on their minds already. I worked with a brilliant 1st on the series *Sensitive Skin*, Steve Roberts, who would automatically fill me in on the sequence of shots that were coming up. Steve had been an actor, so understood the value of that information to me.

# WORKING WITH YOUR OPERATOR

Here's something I'll be doing many times in a day's shoot: I've rehearsed the scene and now I'm working with the camera to line up the shots. I want to know the size of a particular shot. The operator is checking the shot through the camera, I'll look down the lens at him/her and drop my hand down to where I think the bottom of the frame will be. Waist height? Just under the chin? The operator will pop their head out from the eyepiece and show me on their own body exactly where the bottom of the frame is. That's it, nothing is said; it's quick, effortless shorthand. I don't have to waste anyone's time, but now I know the size of the frame. The fact is that, when I'm shooting, I'm thinking in frames. What is the size of the frame that I'm working in? Not only top to bottom but also sometimes side to side, so that I have a sense of what it is that I'm creating with my operator. It's second nature to me now, and it gives me a great sense of concentration and connection to the camera, knowing and feeling the parameters of what we're shooting. Invariably, before a take, I'll look at the lens, reminding myself of my relative relationship to it, my angle, how I'm approaching it, my connection to it.

# HITTING MARKS

Marks are there to keep you in focus and to ensure that the framing or composition of each shot works. There are some marks that are more critical than others, some marks where you have to be spot-on and some less so. If there are a few actors in the same frame, for instance, at different distances from the camera, this can make hitting marks quite critical, since the focus will need to be split between them.

It's quite possible that you could have several marks to hit in one scene.

I quite often count the number of steps between marks, and then repeat them a few times back and forward, between the marks, with the dialogue. I'll be doing this while the crew are busy on the set, adjusting lights, whatever, until my feet get used to the pattern of the marks. It's like any other technical challenge: it gets easier with experience. There are, however, a couple of things you *can* do to take the pressure from your feet, because the last thing you want is to be looking down for your marks during a take.

If the floor isn't in shot and you're having any trouble hitting a mark, you can ask for a sausage. This is a small sausage-shaped sandbag that can be gaffer-taped onto your mark or marks so that when you feel the sausage with your toes, you know you're on your mark. You can, however, find other marks for yourself at eye level. It might be the corner of a table, the edge of a chair, or when you come level with a window.

Again, this takes the pressure off your feet in the takes. Sometimes in a wide shot, any marks may be visible to the camera, so you can't have any, or make do with small pieces of gaffer tape that have to blend in with the floor. If you're in an interior, with a carpet,

69

you may be able to find something in the pattern to give you an invisible mark. In an exterior scene, a field or a street where we can't have visible marks, I'll throw down a stick or a stone to give me a mark that blends in with the location. Marks that you can find at eye level in these circumstances are, of course, very useful. Once you're into close-ups and your feet are out of the frame, the marks can be as visible as you like.

They are beginning to use ready-made marks these days, which are just a bit thicker than gaffer tape on its own and which you can actually feel with your feet, this is a big help.

Let's say that you're shooting an exterior with another actor and you have a mark to hit that's a few feet from the camera, but you're starting the dialogue say a hundred metres away. In order to find out your start position, you turn around so that your heels are on the mark, then walk away from the camera, doing the dialogue at the same pace as you will in the take, stop when you've got to the right point in the dialogue, turn back around, and now you're in the correct start position – get a mark put down there. Rehearse it once or twice for yourselves, and now you're secure.

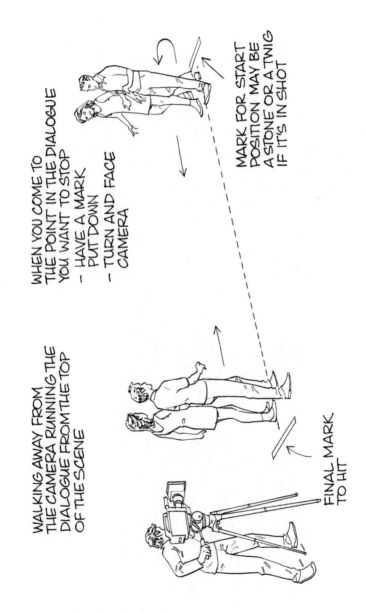

WALKING AWAY FROM
THE CAMERA RUNNING THE
DIALOGUE FROM THE TOP
OF THE SCENE

WHEN YOU COME TO
THE POINT IN THE DIALOGUE
YOU WANT TO STOP

- HAVE A MARK
  PUT DOWN
- TURN AND FACE
  CAMERA

MARK FOR START
POSITION MAY BE
A STONE OR A TWIG
IF IT'S IN SHOT

FINAL MARK
TO HIT

# ROCKING IN

Close-ups can get tricky sometimes if you have to arrive in the frame and hit a mark for a close shot. It *can* be critical that you are precisely on your mark. In this situation, I'll quite often rock in.

I'll put my feet on the mark then lean out of shot, i.e. out of the frame, leaving one foot behind on the mark (my operator will check this for me). On 'Action!', I'll simply lean, sway, rock back into the frame. Now I have no worries or distractions about being off my mark in the close-up, and I can concentrate on the dialogue and performance. Sometimes your fellow actor (whose back is to the camera) will rock in with you, this gives a nice bit of movement in the frame at the start of the shot and that can be very useful in the edit. In fact, I'll often suggest rocking in for just that reason.

MARK

# DIFFERENT TYPES OF CAMERA

There are certain circumstances when we're released from the whole issue of marks: that's when they decide to shoot hand-held or use a Steadicam.

Hand-held is, I guess, self-explanatory. It's when the operator takes the camera off the dolly and has it on his/her shoulder. This is a stylistic choice that the director will make, possibly in conjunction with his operator, to give a certain energy and feel to particular scenes or indeed for the whole piece.

Some years ago I was in a television production called *Other People's Children*, a four-part drama for the BBC. It was a domestic piece that at first sight I wasn't too sure about. However, we worked in a very interesting way. We'd rehearse a scene with the director, Peter Travis. There would be no marks and really no fixed moves. Then we'd step off: after they'd lit the scene, we'd come back on and immediately do a take with the DOP, who also operated, shooting hand-held. He was quite brilliant and stuck to us like a limpet wherever we went on the set. This gave us great spontaneity and freedom – and therefore gave the piece as a whole both energy and spontaneity.

When I see a Steadicam appear on a set, I still get a bit excited. Usually there is a separate Steadicam operator. They'll be wearing a substantial harness with a lot of support on the back (it's a heavy piece of equipment); at the front of the harness is an articulated arm, which the camera itself is attached to. This arm will keep the camera steady no matter where the operator has to go, and there's a small monitor mounted below the camera that the operator uses during a take instead of an eyepiece. They can follow you along a corridor, up a flight of stairs, into another set of rooms and back down again, all in one take, with no tracks, and possibly no marks to hit. It's a wonderful piece of equipment that has really freed up the possibilities of what you can do in a take. A Steadicam has an altogether smoother (steadier) feel to it than hand-held, and, as a result, the viewer is much less aware of it.

The Steadicam.

The body mount is a variation on the Steadicam. As you can see, it's actually attached to the actor and faces back towards them. It's certainly been used in some music videos.

Actor Natasha O'Keeffe with a bodymount.

I talked to Natasha O'Keeffe about her experience working with this piece of kit. It was used in this instance for a fight sequence. Natasha found it quite heavy to wear. She had to kneel on the ground, on a crash mat (a thick rubber mattress used for falls in action shots), she was also wearing kneepads. A couple of the crew were holding the harness from behind so that the camera didn't touch the ground. Her fellow actor wasn't there so she had to pretend to attack him, throwing punches across the camera as though she was on the ground on top of him. In this situation, you might well be playing straight down the lens or just off it, so a piece of white gaffer tape on the lens hood would be very useful to keep your eye-line steady.

Natasha said her back was pretty sore for a few days afterwards but she really enjoyed the experience and felt it was worth it for the impact the shot made in that sequence. I think you'd normally be upright with this so there'd be less strain on the back.

I can see that it could also be used in quite different circumstances, like for an intimate feel on a walking shot, either a single or a two-shot, where you would normally have to build a track or use a Steadicam.

Here's another great piece of equipment I've only just come across but it has been around in different forms for a number of years: the Octocopter.

As you can see from the photograph, it's a small, remote-controlled helicopter, with eight rotors. There are also six- and four-rotor versions (hexa and quad). It can be controlled from a handset, or can be locked into a GPS system to follow a fixed path or indeed to follow a vehicle with a GPS on board. The DOP, director and anyone else on the crew can watch the shots on an iPad.

It's a very flexible piece of hardware that can fly up to 1,000ft (though the legal maximum in the UK is 400ft), then follow the action below or even take panoramic shots. The batteries give a flying time of around ten minutes depending on the weight of the camera used. The camera you see here is pretty compact, but such are the advances with HD that it will match the picture quality of much larger cameras. There are two operators: one controlling the flight, the other the camera, but it can be programmed for a flight with no operators involved. The hardware on board is sending constant information back to the operators in flight. The camera can be tilted and panned through 360 degrees remotely, as it flies. There are larger versions that can take even more advanced cameras.

Whenever you see a proper helicopter shot, you have to appreciate that it costs money to hire such an expensive piece of gear with the pilot included, but the Octocopter makes it possible to get the kind of aerial shots that are usually only possible on a big movie.

You could find yourself doing a running shot, with it first tracking you at eye level, then taking off and sweeping up 200 feet or so to show you running from a bird's-eye view.

If you want to check out more details on the Octocopter, here's the address of the company that I met on a recent shoot, www.cloud12.co.uk.

# LENSES

There are actors who take pride in the fact that they can tell the size of the shot by the size of the lens being used, and, of course, a good technical knowledge is invaluable, but the size of the lens is not the only factor. It also depends on the distance the camera is from you.

The first time I ever asked an operator about lenses, he explained it very simply: the bigger the lens, the closer the shot. Lenses vary in size from 5.9mm (sometimes called a fish-eye lens), through many interim sizes all the way up to 1,000mm and longer. 5.9mm would be a very wide shot, but if it's close enough to you it will distort your face, making your nose protrude and your eyes widen, an effect which may be used to create a particular image for the emotional state of a character. There's a very good illustration of this in *It's a Wonderful Life* – a very close shot on Jimmy Stewart, in total panic.

You double the lens sizes from a 16mm or HD camera, to a 35mm movie camera, e.g. a 16mm lens (a medium-wide angle) on a 16mm or HD camera would be a 32mm or a 35mm camera to achieve the same shot.

Lenses are classified as either 'wide' or 'long'.

- On a 35mm (movie camera), from 5.9mm to 40mm lenses are termed wide and beyond that, long.

- On a 16mm or HD camera, up to a 16mm lens is considered wide, and anything above that long.

- Wide lenses have a wider field of vision and also a greater depth of field or depth of focus.

- Long lenses have a narrower field of vision and a shorter depth of field, the bigger they get.

- Longer, means, in reality, a longer lens barrel, and more glass in it to magnify the image, bringing it closer.

This depth of field (focus) can affect us directly. If you're being shot on a long lens, the depth of field will be very short, which makes hitting your mark more critical or else you'll be out of focus (blurred) in the shot. Wide lenses don't generally have this issue since the depth of field is more generous. But hitting marks is also to do with the composition of the shot. If you're off your mark, you're not in the frame, or only a bit of you is – not much good to anyone!

Here are some examples: a 200mm lens when the camera is 30ft from the actor will have a depth of field (you'll still be in focus) of 3ft 9ins; hitting your mark, to stay in focus, is therefore not critical (although of course it may well be for the composition of the shot).

Let's say you're shooting a movie, so you're on a 35mm camera, and they're using an 85mm lens. If you were, say, 12ft from the camera, you'd be in a tight, head-and-shoulders close-up. A 600mm lens at the same distance will only have a depth of field of 4 inches. Immediately you can see that being on that mark, for focus, is pretty critical.

By the way, long lenses can be very flattering because the depth of field is so short that your face is in focus but your head is slightly 'soft' (out of focus), so it gives a soft glow around the features. The longer lenses, say 600mm, would not normally be used for a close-up since the image would vibrate too much.

Without wishing to complicate this issue for you too much, depth of field can also be affected by the amount of light on you, and the speed of the film stock that they are using.

On a wide lens you may not need to be bang on your mark as you have a deep enough depth of field to play with: if you're an inch or so off it you would still be in focus. So marks are not just to do with being in the right place in the frame, they are also to do with focus. You can see that you're not just working with the oper-ator but also with the focus puller, who's keeping your image clear and sharp in any shot – unless, of course, the intention is to have you soft in the shot (slightly out of focus) at any time.

Here's an illustration of the depth of field with a long lens.

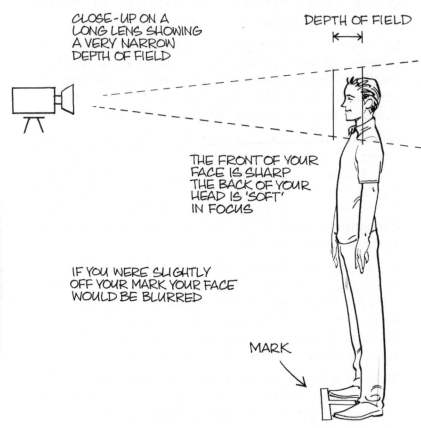

Please don't worry if all this is a bit too technical for you. The fact of the matter is that you may need to go again because you weren't on your mark, and that's that. It's a very common occurrence, and no one on the unit will think much about it, no one will think you're a schmuck – you just go again, probably with a trusty sausage at your feet. And remember, you may be able to rock in!

# THE FRAME

This concept of working in frames means that whatever happens outside the frame is irrelevant, even if it's a matter of only a few centimetres. Stewart Granger was a big Hollywood star in the fifties and sixties: British, handsome, and with a wonderful mane of grey hair. In one movie he was playing a classical violinist, so there was a sequence of concert footage, with some intense close-ups of him in full flow. To achieve this they had a close shot of Granger, but underneath him (out of the frame) was a man kneeling doing the fingering, and on the other side (also out of the frame), another man kneeling, doing the bowing, and immediately below, a third man (out of the frame), holding up the violin, with Granger emoting away, *in* the frame, pretending to play!

Of course, this is quite an extreme illustration, but imagine dealing with all that and still managing to get a performance on the take. This idea of the frame can be an enormous help in focusing your performance, no matter what bizarre situations you find yourself in.

The camera just happens to be on and I just happen to walk in front of it. This is the effect that I'm invariably trying to achieve on camera. One of the things I try to avoid is walking into the frame, hitting my mark and saying my first line of dialogue. If I have to either enter or leave the frame, particularly in a wider shot, I may be interested not only in the height of the frame I'm working in, but sometimes the breadth. Again, my operator can give me this information and I may well have marks put down showing me the edges of the frame, so that I know exactly when I'm entering or exiting. I'll start my first line just out of the frame and throw my last line away just as I'm leaving it. This helps escape that 'stagey' feeling that I'm constantly trying to avoid, making it look more 'accidental'. Now, there are exceptions to this, with certain types of comedy or very intense scenes, where you want to punctuate a moment deliberately.

When I'm leaving a frame it may well be more interesting, rather than moving out directly to the left or the right, to exit quite close to the lens. In other words, you walk towards the camera and then just skim down one side of it. You may be asked to exit the frame, 'camera left' or 'camera right'. But since you are facing the camera, you'll need to reverse that instruction, since 'camera left' and 'right' is from the camera's point of view. If you exit camera right, that's your left. Camera left is your right.

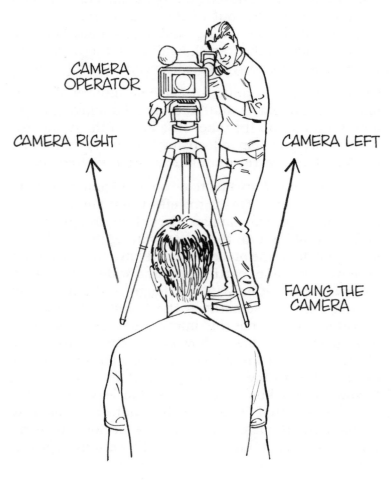

# THE BANANA

I was on set with a young actor recently, and told him about my book. 'Have you mentioned the banana?' And he told me this story.

A young actress he knew had her first ever day on a set.

She had to walk towards the camera and exit the frame close to one side of it. She was asked to give them a banana on her way out. So as she approached the camera, she pretended to slip. 'Okay, hold it! CUT! What are you doing?' 'Well you wanted me to do a banana,' she said. She'd assumed banana – skin – slip. Fair enough if you've never heard such a strange request.

Let me therefore illuminate the banana.

There are occasions when you will be asked for the above. But all it means is that instead of walking in a straight line towards the camera or possibly a fellow actor, you'll put a slight curve into that move. This may be to do with the camera trying to avoid the edge of a set, or a lamp or some other object if you're on location. Or it may be because you're masking another actor at that point in the take.

It's a simple enough thing to do, the audience won't be aware of it since the lens is moving with you and you'll find you can easily achieve it without it looking odd or forced.

*Et voilà...* the banana.

# WINDING UP FOR THE TAKE

If I'm about to do a take, where I'm entering a room or set from an exterior, I'll be thinking about my journey into that scene. Did I walk along a street? Come up a flight of stairs? As they're running up to the take – 'Turn over! Sound running! Camera set!' – I'll be jumping up and down on the spot, exhaling heavily, pushing the breath out of my lungs. This achieves a couple of things. This slight sense of breathlessness helps to convey that journey, but once I've achieved that sense of physical activity, I'll do my best to control it through the take; I'll try *not* to show it. It may well make me break and pause in the dialogue in slightly different places, helping that sense of naturalism that I'm striving for. If there's a flight of stairs off the set then I'll use them to run up and into the take.

I find this useful, too, for certain emotional scenes; the need to suppress that breathlessness can help me feel that I'm suppressing anger, fear, etc. It also quite simply pumps adrenalin through the body and helps get me up there for the take. Filming can be a rather passive activity physically, and although I'm searching for relaxation and stillness, I'm also looking for a dynamic concentration underneath that. It's certainly not something I'm going to be doing for every take, far from it, but I do find it a useful tool to have at my disposal. By the way, if some of the crew think it's a bit weird, so be it. Who wants to be normal? Weird is good!

I picked this tip up from the late Bob Peck, who'd do press ups before a take, to give him extra intensity. I also watched Joe Mawle use even more extreme forms of physical wind-up when he was playing Jesus in *The Passion*. All that matters at the end of the day is what's seen in the frame. How you get into that frame, that take, is your business. Whatever works for you... do it.

While the crew are preparing for the take, you don't need to stay stuck on your mark. Once the shot is lined up, you can walk away from the lens, concentrating on the scene, and then walk back in just before they call 'Action!' That small physical activity can help your energy and concentration. If I'm in a close-up and, for technical reasons, it's impossible to come off the mark, then I'll drop my eyes in the run up so that, on 'Action!', I'm lifting my eyes up into the lens. This gives the eyes intention and energy.

# HOLDING BACK THE MACHINE

When a film unit is chasing its arse, working to a tight schedule (which is more and more the norm in modern television but can also apply to low-budget features), trying to get a certain number of pages in the can in any one day, the pressure can get pretty intense or the director and the entire crew. It's very much the 1st AD's job to keep the great lumbering beast of the unit moving, and that includes the director: the 1st AD will often push the director, letting him know just how long he's got to get a particular shot or scene done. He/she should do this subtly, i.e. quietly… The last thing I need as an actor is to know what the time is or how long we have left to get a take done. I've enough to think about. In fact, I hate to know the time when I'm shooting. I want to suspend myself in the moment. If I'm about to do a take and I'm told it's only half an hour till lunch, that could very easily disrupt my concentration: now I'm thinking about cod and chips when I'm in the middle of a take… not the best bit of motivation.

It can be very easy to pick up on this urgency and get rushed into a take that I'm not quite ready for. I can find myself being checked by costume and make-up and hearing the 1st AD shout, 'Okay! And turn over!' (This means, turn on the camera and the sound, we're going for a take.) But if I'm not quite there or nowhere near it, I'll just say, very calmly, to my 1st AD, 'Sorry, I'm not ready yet, give me a minute,' or something like that. The same applies if I'm running the lines for myself before the take, checking something in my script or just getting my concentration. I want to go into the take when I'm ready for it: there's nothing worse than being rushed; worrying about something that's outside the scene I'm shooting, that's niggling at my concentration while I'm in front of the camera.

# STOPPING A TAKE
## or
# THE SHOW DOES NOT GO ON!

We're British actors and my God we're proud of it! So we should be, and we bring to our work on camera this fearsome discipline from the stage. But we're dealing with a different set of criteria here. If a take goes wrong, if something throws us, someone drops a spanner, coughs, moves in our eye-line, disturbs our concentration, our British actor's impulse is to 'carry on' and make the best of it, just as we'd have to if we were on stage. No! No! No! This is film: *we can stop!* There's nothing worse than getting to the end of a take thinking, 'Shit, that just wasn't right. I was really thrown then.' But you hear the 1st AD and or the director shouting, 'Okay, good, check that – moving on!' So you're standing there full of angst about a crap take, and they're moving the camera! They're on to the next set-up, and you're left for the rest of the day thinking, 'That wasn't right, God, that take was shit.'

86

I've had takes haunt me for days. So if it's going wrong for whatever reason: *stop the fucker!* It's not that big a deal. You just say, 'Sorry, sorry – that noise? What was that? Let me start again.' 1st AD: 'Okay, cut, let's set up to go again and can we have *quiet on the set please*!' Some such dialogue, and you're off again. Just remember that it's only *your* face on the screen, not the guy who dropped the spanner. The audience don't know about him; they don't know he fucked your concentration and that's why you weren't quite on the ball in that scene. *Stopping* is common as shit. Just *do it.*

When you become more experienced, you can, if it feels right, say, 'Keep rolling, I'll pick it up.' In other words, you may have blown a line or been distracted but, rather than break concentration, you stay in the moment. Camera and sound don't cut; everything stays running: you pick up the dialogue from where you want, and you go again. Now this does take experience and confidence, so it's something to try further down the line. And it's only an alternative to stopping!

This whole sense of urgency can be less prevalent on a properly funded feature. That pressure may not be so intense, although, believe me, these same situations can and do arise on a big feature, and more obviously on low-budget features.

# ASKING FOR ANOTHER TAKE

This can be a tough one to get used to, especially on a television or low-budget movie shoot where they're up against a tight schedule. On a well-financed movie, it can be less of a problem. If you're working with a proper film camera, as opposed to a digital one, you'll reach the end of the take and hear 'Cut! Check it!' from the director. This means that he/she is happy with the take and wants to move on to the next shot. Now, some directors will do you the courtesy of asking if you're happy with the take you've just done, but not many, and particularly not in television. By the way, 'Check it!' means 'check the gate'. The focus puller will remove the lens on the front of the camera and shine a little pencil torch into it. Generally he/she will say, 'The gate's clear!' or 'The gate's good!' but occasionally, you'll hear this: 'Hair in the gate!' The immediate response from the 1st AD or the director will be, 'We're going again!' and you'll set up for another take. The word 'hair' doesn't necessarily mean that there is actually hair or dust in the gate of the camera. It's more likely a shaving of emulsion from the film (or 'stock', as it's referred to), is lodged in the gate. The result would be that, when that footage is viewed in the editing process, you could see what looks like a piece of hair, wriggling across the screen. If you get a lot of hairs, it means that the stock itself is faulty and may need to be replaced, but whatever the cause, if there's a hair in the gate, there's no discussion: you go again.

You'll never hear 'Check the gate!' with an HD camera: they'll simply call 'Cut!', make sure the sound and camera departments are happy and 'Okay, moving on!' – which means they're about to move the camera for the next shot, and you have even less time to ask for that other take. The sooner you ask, the better, before they move that camera. I've trained myself, over many years, to assess a take immediately. As soon as we've cut, I'll be running that take back in my head, making sure I'm happy. If not, I'm asking for another one straight away. On occasion, an experienced director may ask me what the problem was, I might mention a particular line and he/she may reassure me that they won't be on me, or using that bit of that take in the final edit. Wide shots, for instance, are rarely used all the way through a scene. They're there to establish the geography of the characters and the location and may well be used only at the beginning and the end of a scene for a few seconds. If I feel that they're talking sense, I'll let it go and move on. However, even though I know they're up against a tough schedule, I may well hold my ground and try for another one. The average take is not long, and by the time you've stood around and argued the toss you could have got another one in the can. The cost of that disk/hard drive is much cheaper than film stock, and that can be a consideration in your favour.

You have to remember that, when scenes are edited, you won't necessarily be in vision for every line of dialogue you have. That would be a very boring way to edit. Watch any movie/television scene and you'll be aware that quite often they will be on an actor's face who has no dialogue or they may well cut to another actor in the middle of someone else's line. Be that as it may, you do want your takes to be as good as you can get them and walk away at the end of the day feeling that you got at least one good take in the can for each set-up. Now, on a soap, like *EastEnders* or *Coronation Street*, it could be tougher to get that other take: you might really have to stand your ground. These productions are shot at such a rate, I have no great advice for you in these circumstances: it may well be a matter of how tough you are, I'm afraid. On a four- or six-part televison drama, it does become a bit easier. At the end of the day it can all come down to the personalities involved; some directors can deal with the intense pressure of a schedule and not pass on their stress to the actors and some... can't.

# MID-SHOTS AND CLOSE-UPS

Once the wide shot is in the can, they'll be moving onto mid-shots and close-ups. If I have a lot of dialogue in the scene compared with the other actors, I may well request that they shoot my close-ups first. This may be impossible for technical reasons, but if I can go first, I much prefer it. There's a danger that constant repetition of dialogue and performance off-camera (this is when the camera is on your fellow actors and you are not in shot) can result in your getting stale and tired. You can literally blow your performance on the wrong side of the camera. I've done it in the past, been working away off-camera, honing the speeches and the scene for anything up to an hour or more only to find, when they finally got to my shots, that I'd peaked and couldn't get it back. The fact is it could literally be hours before they get to your close-ups... *hours*! They could get the wide in by, say, 11.30 a.m., and then be shooting on the other actors. Remember, they have to relight each time for each set of close shots, so you can be sent off the set a few times while this happens. Then, what do you know, it's *lunch*! You try really hard not to stuff your face then you're back on set again. Maybe you don't get to your close shots until 3.30 p.m. – perfectly possible, believe me – and you've been repeating that dialogue so brilliantly for four hours! So now you barely know what it means and who you're playing. That's why I'd rather get in there while it's fresh so that I'm still finding it, discovering it on the takes.

There's this British actor's thing that we must 'be there' for each other and, of course, you do want to give your fellow actors what they need for their close shots. On the other hand, you want to be fresh for your own close shots. The answer, I think, is to be constantly aware of the sequence of the work ahead, and pace yourself accordingly.

To be frank – I'm still working on this one.

When you do get to your close shots, you may well not be running the whole scene but coming in later in the dialogue, and they may well cut on the shot before the scene is finished. A line will be suggested by the director or script supervisor to start the take. In which case, I may well suggest that we go a few lines back from this so that I can get into the scene before we hit that point, so that when the take actually starts, I'll already be in full flow. You may find this doesn't work for you, but invariably I prefer that run-in.

# CLOSE-UPS AND EYE-LINES

As we move from wide shots to mid-shots and close-ups, the positions for the actors may shift and change a bit in order to accommodate new camera positions. As we go through this process, I'll be thinking of my eyes getting progressively closer to the lens. This really becomes an issue in close-ups, when I'll be literally flirting with the lens. I'll want my fellow actors to be as close to the lens as possible; then I'll use the off-camera actor's eye nearest to the lens to focus on, so that my eyes are just missing the lens. This makes the shot more powerful and allows the camera to really read what's going on in my eyes. It also keeps the eyes very still in the shot, unless, of course, there are emotional reasons why I'd want more movement in my eyes – fear, or excitement, for instance. There may be occasions when getting the off-camera actor that close isn't appropriate. If it doesn't match the previous shot, for example, the operator will let me know and we'll adjust the eye-line (the position of the off-camera actor) accordingly.

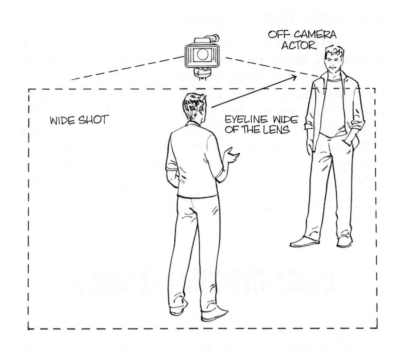

OFF CAMERA ACTOR

WIDE SHOT

EYELINE WIDE OF THE LENS

OFF CAMERA ACTOR MOVES RIGHT INTO THE LENS FOR THE CLOSE-UP

EYELINE IN THE CLOSE-UP NICE AND TIGHT TO THE LENS USING THE EYE CLOSEST TO THE LENS

CLOSE-UP

If I can't quite see my fellow actor (this can happen if everything has been moved around so much that he or she can't get in there for you), I may ask for a piece of white gaffer to be put on the lens hood of the camera, and I'll play not to my fellow actor but to the mark. I've even had gaffer put on the shoulder of my operator. The gaffer on the lens hood is also very useful if you're left alone at the end of a scene, as it gives you a completely steady focus. Indeed, a mark to concentrate on in an extreme close-up can really help the emotional intention for the shot. Of course, this is very technical stuff – maybe something to be thought of and tried out further down the line. If it doesn't work for you, abandon it immediately and come back to it at some later date. It may not work for you at all, and that's fine too.

Gaffer tape on the lens hood.    Gaffer tape on the operator's shoulder.

# KEEPING YOUR EYE-LINES CLEAR

There are a lot of personnel on a unit. There can be upwards of twenty to thirty people standing around while you're doing a take. It can be very distracting as you focus on your fellow actor, who is off-camera, that just behind him is a spark who's been asked to hold a lamp, or indeed any member of the crew who may just 'be there'. It's a difficult enough job anyway, keeping your imagination flowing, functioning in this disjointed, fractured way of working, without having a crew member staring you in the face or just standing there picking their nose. How to handle it? You can of course *stop*! Ask the crew member to move or duck down out of sight, or you can turn to your trusty 1st AD and ask him quietly to clear your eye-line. I have on occasion asked my director to move. He/she will be huddled round a monitor with cans on, with the script super-viser and a couple of other interested parties, so you have this little knot of people watching you while you're doing your take, and it can be very distracting if they are right in your eye-line. They'll be blissfully unaware because they are all intent on doing their jobs, but that's no good if they are getting in the way of yours. The monitor is on a trolley and can be easily moved to another part of the set. It's obviously more productive if you spot this in the last rehearsal before the take; then you can check it out with the 1st before the take itself. There are also instances when I've asked my 1st to clear the set of anyone who doesn't really need to be there. This could be for a very emotional scene where we need all the concentration we can muster. It can also begin to feel a bit theatrical if you feel you've got an 'audience'. Everyone's there to do their best job, but there are a lot of people on a crew, and it's very possible that once they've done what's necessary they can step off the set. This is usually done automatically for bed/sex scenes, but if it's not, again – that quiet word with your 1st.

# BED SCENES

Since I've brought it up (well, someone had to), let's look at sex on camera. Of course, it's all very exciting, jumping into bed with someone you don't know or know only in a professional way, but on a *set*, in front of a crew of twenty to thirty people, it can be very nerve-racking. I think it may well be tougher on women, since it's rare for a male actor to be 'full frontal' on screen – on camera, women tend to be more exposed than men.

A sex scene is something that I want to rehearse – and I'm being very serious here. The last thing you want is to throw yourself at each other, generally writhe around and hope for the best. It needs to be choreographed like a dance, so that you know from moment to moment where your legs, arms, hands, heads and mouths are going. This can all be done with clothes on: a tracksuit is best. It should be a closed set (completely private, with just the actors and the director), and it needs time: time to explore the movements, the mood you want to create, the shapes you want to make. You want that feeling of filling the frame with interesting body shapes, like a moving sculpture. It needs sensitivity from the director and from the actors, a sense of being careful with each other. Once you have a shape on it, it'll help you during the take to concentrate on what you've rehearsed. You'll feel less self-conscious and more at ease. Once you've arrived at what you're after, then the DOP will work out the shots with the director. That closed set should be maintained while you're shooting. Of course, some crew members will need to be there but the 1st should make sure that it's kept to a minimum. If you feel this isn't the case, then have a quiet word with the 1st to clear the set of anyone who isn't required.

You might be a couple of hours shooting a scene like this and, by the time you've got it in the can, you'll have used a lot of purely sexual energy, and it can leave you feeling quite exhausted. A sense of anti-climax, quite literally. Again, be aware of what you're eating beforehand and make sure you take a toothbrush into work, maybe some mints or breath-freshener: this all helps you to feel a bit more physically confident in that very intimate situation.

You should find the wardrobe department very good here: they'll be hovering with an essential dressing gown as soon as they hear 'Cut!', or as soon as you get out of bed. The anticipation of being completely naked is (in my experience) worse than the actual event. The crew are very sensitive to these issues, and I've always found myself wondering after the first couple of minutes: why the hell are all these people wearing clothes? This is so much more comfortable!

# LISTENING AND REACTION SHOTS

Let's say that you're shooting a big dinner scene, with six to eight characters around a table. It's a couple of pages long, but you only have two lines in the entire scene. Be aware when you start on a dinner scene like this, it can really take a long time to shoot with a lot of repetition. Also be aware that if you're eating in the scene, you'll be eating the same amounts for hours... so do you want that big lunch or breakfast?... Do you? On occasion, if I've been eating a lot in a scene like this I've asked for a bucket by my chair and spat the food out at the end of each take; not, of course, a very edifying spectacle but better that than getting to the end of it feeling bloated and sick!

You've done the wide shots, maybe a few two-shots, then they start picking up some singles. It's very common, on your close-ups, that the other actors at the table will be moved around and bunched up at one end in order to help your eye-line, i.e. keeping your eyes close to the lens. This can throw you a bit if you're not used to it. Suddenly, when the pressure is on you and you want to be at your most relaxed and effective, all the geography of the wide shot is moved around leaving you a bit disorientated. This can happen in any kind of scene, by the way, not just around a table.

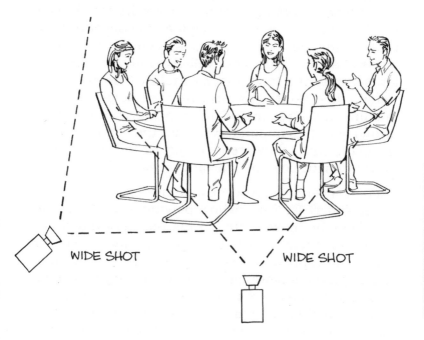

WIDE SHOT          WIDE SHOT

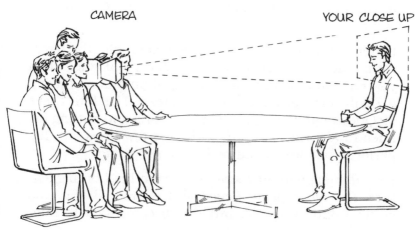

CAMERA          YOUR CLOSE UP

So the camera comes on to you for your close-up, and the scene is run.

It can be very easy in this situation to feel, with all that focus on you, that you need to *do* something, but what *do* you do when you listen? Watch friends socially when they're listening: mostly that's all they do... They *do nothing... nothing.* You have your subtext in your head for the scene you're playing, so concentrate on that... Just *be...* Just *listen.* Remember that these kinds of shots, in the edit, will generally be used for a few seconds at a time; that's certainly true in conventional edits. So it's not necessary or advisable to be pushing and straining. Watch any movie or television drama with this in mind. What are the actors doing in the shots when they are listening, or indeed *reacting*, to what might be quite startling news?

There is a very useful scene in a movie called *Sleepers* when Robert De Niro, who's playing a priest, is told that boys he looked after in his neighbourhood and known all their lives had been sexually abused for months in a prison for young offenders. It's shocking and distressing news for him to hear. He just listens, he's still, he *does nothing*, and that's what gives the take its intensity. I read in a rare interview that De Niro considers that some of his best takes are when he is thinking about something else, so: *there are no rules.*

I often think that on stage as well as on film the hardest moments are when you *don't* have dialogue, when you have to rely on your concentration and on having a really firm grasp of your subtext. The late Steve McQueen had the reputation of cutting and cutting his lines in a script, so that, with very few lines left, his performance was contained in him *reacting*.

He famously had only several lines in his first big feature *The Magnificent Seven* and wondered if it was worth taking the role, but the director said to him,

'Don't worry, I'll give you the camera.' In other words, his performance would be in his *reaction* shots – and when you watch the movie, it's all there by the bucketload. Again in *Bullitt*, McQueen's dialogue is minimal, but his concentration is wonderful and riveting to watch.

# SOUND

When you get into singles (single close-ups), the sound department will invariably ask you not to overlap the dialogue. This is for the editing process where they need your lines *clean* of any dialogue from the other actors. The challenge here is that, along with the other actors, you've built up a nice rhythm to the scene and now, when it comes to those crucial close-ups, that rhythm is broken; those nice overlaps you developed and that moment when you came in really hard on that cue aren't allowed, so you have to remember and/or imagine those rhythms and that energy but play each line in isolation. I still find this tricky sometimes; I love pace on a scene and find it hard to slow myself up. In fact, one of my criteria for a scene beginning to work, as we rehearse, is that it begins to feel shorter; suddenly the scene's over before you realise it, and it's then that I feel it's starting to cook. One advantage here is that you can take time to come in on your line, when it feels right to you. Of course, it's going to feel very slow, but all of these pauses will be taken out in the edit and the original pace of the scene will hopefully be restored when it's finally cut together. The fact is that a good editor can improve the pace and energy of a scene.

# WATCHING PLAYBACK

All cameras, be they film or digital, have the facility to instantly play back a take on the director's and the DOP's monitors. It's very common for a director to review a take, and they may well invite the actors to have a look too, out of courtesy and interest, or to help explain a point they're trying to make. Unless it's really essential, I avoid this.

When I was starting out in movies, it was the norm at the end of the day for everyone to sit in some makeshift screening room and watch the rushes (the takes) from the previous day. This was essentially for the director, the editor, the DOP and script supervisor to discuss various takes and keep track of how the work was progressing, but it was open to everyone involved. I was always very keen to be there, and I took this habit into my television work too, always wanting to see whatever I could of what we'd shot. I have to say, now that this is not the case. I'm much more confident of the effect I'm having on camera and don't want to make myself feel in the least self-conscious about how I look or about my performance. When I was younger, I guess it was part of my learning curve to see if what I'd intended was actually there.

Nowadays, thanks to the advent of digital technology, the director can sit in his/her hotel room and see what they have in the can. It's a much more 'private practice' now. I worked with a terrific young director recently who had the day's takes sent to his iPad. If you want to see the footage of what you've shot, then ask the director or the producer. It may well be possible.

At the end of the day, if it helps you and you're offered the opportunity... do it. I read recently that the wonderful Jeff Bridges watches every take he does on playback, so whatever works for you. If it makes you self-conscious... avoid!

There are actually small monitors all over the place on a film set: the grip will have one on the dolly (very useful to him during takes); the sound mixer will have one; and there are always small screens attached to the top of the camera itself. Watch out for these: they're on a mount that swivels round. There have been occasions when I've gone into a take with that monitor staring straight at me. If I can actually see myself in the middle of a take, I find this really distracting so I'll – *stop*! Just keep your eye on that monitor and make sure that it's turned away from you towards the operator.

# CONTINUITY

The script supervisor is responsible for continuity. They were known, up until a few years ago, as 'the continuity woman'. I'm not sure why the change in job description came about, but there it is. I've never come across a man who does this job, by the way, it's always been a woman. Perhaps having an eye for every detail of movement on the set is a particularly female attribute; it's certainly a job that I don't envy.

As I've discussed, coverage varies from one shot for the entire scene (Woody Allen works this way a lot) to multiple angles and tracking shots galore. Apart from watching props and any action, the script supervisor has to keep careful notes on all those angles and set-ups (different positions for the camera); quite possibly pulling the director up if she feels that one particular shot won't work with another in the edit. These notes will be essential to the director and the editor when they come to cut the film together. She is, in fact, the

101

middleman between the director and the editor; it's a very demanding job.

Let's take the example of the 'dinner round the table' scenario, where all the actors are eating and drinking. Once you've done the wide shot and they come into those two-shots and singles, you'll have to match your actions from the wide shots with those in the closer ones. For instance, you have a line: 'What time did you arrive?' In the wide shot, you took a drink of wine at the end of that line, so you'll have to 'match that' in your close shots, i.e. take your drink in exactly the same place. If the scene is a couple of pages long, with a fair amount of dialogue, and you're eating and drinking throughout, perhaps using a napkin as well as a knife, fork and a glass, you'll have to replicate all of these small actions from the wide shot in the close. This is all to do with the editing process. When they are cutting the film together, they can't cut from the wide to the close and possibly back to wide again if you're not consistent with those actions.

The props department will be in and out constantly, keeping drinks to the same level and replacing food that's been eaten, making sure that cutlery and napkins are reset between each take.

Once the actions in the wide have been established, I'll be going over them again, quietly with the lines, while they're setting up for my close shots.

It's perfectly possible that you'll do a take and the script supervisor will come over and say something like, 'Look, you put your fork down in the middle of the line on the word "thrilled"… You were late with the fork that time.' This kind of detail can still sometimes throw me, but it's very common. You do develop a memory for these things as you become more experienced, but continuity can still get me a bit pissed off on a set.

One of the theatrical skills that's helped me enormously with my film work is mime. I've done quite a lot of mime, movement-oriented, physical theatre and dance in my career. This has all helped me to develop a strong visual memory with the ability to consistently reproduce intricate, detailed movement. It's also given me a strong 'spacial awareness' when I'm working/ blocking scenes with my fellow actors and the camera. And it's been a big help with hitting marks, since dancing has made me more aware of my feet.

Smoking is one of the greatest 'acting props' of all time (what a pity that it kills you). The amount of information you can get across, with the whole business of lighting up, when and how you inhale, when and how you exhale, that lovely grey mist of smoke around your face... Christ, it's brilliant! Smoking also gives you the effect of 'split focus', since you have this activity to concentrate on through the scene. It can help give a real sense of naturalism. But these small movements and punctuations during the dialogue can be difficult to match from the wide to the close, so do be aware that, if you choose to smoke through a scene, you could be smoking for hours! Literally. I've had occasions when I've been green by the time we wrapped on a scene I've chosen to smoke through. There can be another problem these days: the powers that be don't want to be seen to be encouraging smoking on screen. This happened when I was shooting a five-parter, *Marchlands*, set in 1968 when smoking was everywhere. Having established that the character smoked, I was then asked to cut it back for those PC reasons. Irritating? Well, yes. Had they seen *Mad Men*?

But continuity isn't always God. There are occasions when the director will say to the script supervisor, 'It doesn't matter, it's an either/or' – meaning that the director will be on the wide or the close shot at that particular point in the edit, so continuity will be irrelevant. That tends to be the end of the matter and we can move on.

# COMING IN LATE OR FOR A ONE-SCENE PART

Coming in for a one-scene part is actually quite a tough thing to do. It's much easier if you're in every day, playing a big fat role and getting into the rhythm of the shoot. Coming in late to the shoot and only being on for one or two days can be like trying to get onto a moving train. If possible, try to get to the shoot a day early. If it's on location, ask if you can travel a day early or get there early enough on your first day to spend time on the set before you're called. You could do this through your agent or, when the 2nd AD phones you with your call time, tell them that this is what you'd like to do. If I'm coming in after a shoot has started, I'll always try to get out to the set early to meet the costume and make-up departments. I'll have already met the costume designer but not their assistants. If I haven't done it already, I may well try on some costume and wear it for a bit. Then I'll go into the make-up trailer. We'll have spoken on the phone, and I'll have let them know I'm coming out and can we try my make-up? Any decent make-up artist will be happy to do this, assuming they can be spared from the set. There's nothing worse than hitting the make-up chair on your first day at 7 a.m., having your hair and make-up done in a rush without enough discussion, then you're on set by 8 a.m., facing the camera, feeling that you don't look quite right, or you look bloody awful! Already you're off to a bad start. Being able to meet costume and make-up in a less-pressured way is good for everybody.

Then I'll ask the 2nd AD to get me to the set. A runner or 3rd AD will do this. So I walk onto the set, and: *who do I want to meet?* – Exactly.

Once I've said hello to my immediate crew members and anyone else on the crew who I can easily get to, I'll squeeze myself in somewhere and… watch. Maybe for an hour or more. What I'm doing here is feeling the general atmosphere, the 'rhythm' of the shoot. Every shoot has a different rhythm or pace. Does it feel relaxed? A few gags knocking around? Or are the director and the 1st a bit stressed and up against the schedule? How much coverage are they after? Is that pretty conventional or are there lots of different angles and therefore a lot of repetition for the actors? You may not be that aware of what you're taking in, but the great thing is that your first day will now feel a bit more like your second.

If all this is impossible to arrange, try and get to the set for the scene before yours or, if your scene is first thing that morning, try to get to the set a bit ahead of time and take things in. Try to avoid the scenario where you're hiding in your trailer until you're called, then walking straight onto the set and starting to shoot, without having met anyone.

This is aimed at actors with little or no experience, but I've been doing this job for a long time now and it's still my practice.

If you're just starting out: when you're wrapped from your scene and due to leave… *don't*. Check with the 1st; ask if it's okay if you stick around for a while because you're new to this work and it would be helpful to you if you could watch. Unless the set is too cramped to accommodate you, this will be fine. At the very least they'll be impressed that you're keen to learn. Now, watching filming can be like watching paint dry, but do it: you may not be aware of what you're taking in, but when I started out, I always watched – watched rehearsals, for film and stage, watched performances from the wings, every night in some cases. Just watched. There may well be some very experienced actors on your shoot, so you can

105

watch how they handle themselves on the set and with the unit.

In my twenties, I worked on a French film called *Providence* with the wonderful director Alain Resnais. Among a distinguished cast was Dirk Bogarde. He was in his fifties, and one of the most accomplished and skilful movie actors of his generation. I had arrived at the location in Antwerp, straight from the airport, and was introduced to him over lunch. As I sat down, his first words to me were, 'Have you got your expenses?' 'Em, no,' I replied. 'You're not a cunt, are you?' 'Em... no.' 'Well, get your expenses.' After this somewhat startling exchange we chatted happily away, then I realised that he wasn't working that day; he hadn't been called, but was just following the shoot. This was by no means his first day. He'd been shooting for a week or so, I think, but he simply wanted to stay involved, stay 'in there' and... *watch*.

He was also wonderful with the crew. Every morning when he walked onto the set, he would shake hands and say hello to each member of the crew, acknowledging the fact that filming is a collaborative process on every level. So never be afraid to go out to the crew: they work bloody hard and always appreciate our recognition and inclusion.

I learned a great deal from watching and working with Bogarde: his total immersion and concentration, always working on the set, constantly repeating moves and lines before a take; and when I did the same before my close-ups, he fell in with me in my private rehearsal. A great professional and a very charming man (most of the time!).

# WILD AND ATMOS TRACKS

Once you have the whole scene in the can and you're about to move on to the next, it's very common to do some wild tracks. These are lines which for various reasons have been difficult to record properly – usually one or two lines at most, but could be more. The 1st will call, 'Quiet on the set,' the sound man will call, 'Sound running,' no one will call 'Action!', your cue is from the sound man, and then you start in your own time. If it's easier, you can have your script in your hand. You do the required lines with roughly the same inflection and pace as you did in the take. It's not a bad idea to repeat the line two or three times so as to give them some alternatives. I'll quite often suggest this myself: 'Keep running and I'll do two or three.' You'll usually be pretty consistent here, as you've just finished the scene so you're still 'in there'. If you've been walking in, say, a two-handed tracking shot, you might repeat the movement with the boom operator following you so the sense of the journey you're making is still there.

After this, the sound department may well want an atmos track. All that's required from us, and indeed the whole crew, is to be absolutely silent and still for a minute or two. What is happening here is that they want to record the ambient sound of the location. This'll be added as the background atmosphere behind the dialogue as they mix all the sound together in what is called the dub, the part of the post-production process when all the sound is mixed together to create an aural backdrop to the final film.

# CROSSING THE LINE

This particular issue doesn't affect us in terms of per-formance or in the way we work. It's to do with camera positions and the way in which one character relates to another on screen. In the very simplest example: if two actors are facing each other in a scene, and the camera is over the left shoulder of one actor focusing on the other, then, when the camera comes round to the second actor, the camera must be over their right shoulder. In other words, if you draw an imaginery line between the two actors, the camera must stay on the same side of that line at all times. If not, when the edi-tor cuts the scene together, it will look as though both the actors are looking in the same direction and not at each other.

CAMERA OVER
RIGHT SHOULDER ONTO
CLOSE UP OF ACTOR
OPPOSITE

CAMERA OVER
LEFT SHOULDER OF
ONE ACTOR ONTO CLOSE UP
OF THE OTHER

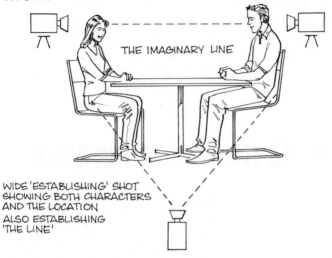

THE IMAGINARY LINE

WIDE 'ESTABLISHING' SHOT
SHOWING BOTH CHARACTERS
AND THE LOCATION
ALSO ESTABLISHING
'THE LINE'

BUT YOU CAN CROSS THE LINE
**IF**
CAMERA TRACKING BEHIND
THE CHARACTERS CROSSING
THE LINE BUT IN VISION
THEREFORE TAKING
THE AUDIENCE WITH YOU TO
THE OTHER SIDE
OF THE LINE

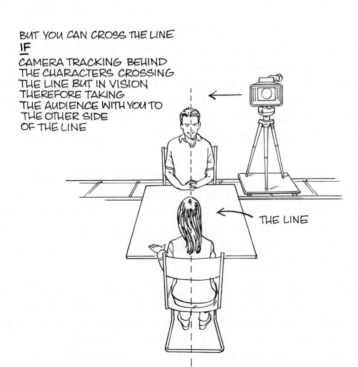

THE LINE

Going back to our old favourite, the dinner scene with several characters, this 'crossing the line' issue can become very complicated, and many a heated discussion can be had between the DOP, the operator, the director and the script supervisor around and about this issue. Luckily for us, it's something we *don't* have to worry about. Now there's a result!

# LOSING THE OFF-CAMERA ACTOR

There are occasions, because of injury, illness or the fact that you've come back to do a pick-up some weeks after you've wrapped the film, when you may not have your fellow actors there at all. It's rare, but it can happen. If so, don't panic! It's not as difficult as it seems.

If you're entirely on your own, then the script supervisor will stand by the camera and read the off-lines. This I do not want: I don't want to be trying to act opposite a non-actor with her head buried in the script, reading the dialogue, however sweet and accommodating she might be. I'll ask her very nicely to step away from the camera, out of my eye-line, to read the lines.

Then I'll have a lighting pole set nice and close to the lens, with a cross made from two pieces of white gaffer tape stuck to it at the same height as the eye-line for my absent actor (selfish bastard). Then I'll play the take to my trusty gaffer that will keep my eyes and my concentration focused.

Dirk Bogarde had to do this in a movie called *The Damned*. He had his close-ups for a big dinner scene to pick up after he'd wrapped. Originally there were sixteen other characters at the table, but for the pick-ups he was totally alone. He had poles and gaffer set around the camera for each character and did the take. The phrase he used to describe that experience has always stayed with me: 'It's my job, it's what I do.' These situations can seem a bit overwhelming but when you understand the process – namely that only the shot matters at the end of the day and that only fragments of that shot will be used in the final edit – it begins to fall into perspective.

I was interested to read in Michael Caine's book, *Acting in Film*, that Orson Welles would choose to do his close-ups with no other actors there at all. I understand this completely: his focus was then only on the shot itself and on his relationship with the camera.

# DRIVING

Make sure that you get some practice in any vehicle you're going to have to drive; that you're comfortable and confident with it. Drive it around a bit, stop and start, check how it brakes and accelerates. Check the seatbelts a few times and how the car starts, so if you have to get in or out in a hurry, you're not held up in the take by these details.

Frankly, shooting in a car can be a bit of a palaver. There are times when you'll be driving with the camera mounted on a bracket by the window, and if it's a two-handed scene, you'll have to repeat it with the camera mounted on the other side of the car for the matching close-up. Then you could easily have the operator crammed in the back seat with the focus puller shooting you from behind to get another angle. This is not the camera department's favourite occupation: it's fiddly, uncomfortable and time-consuming for them.

I've had occasions when the camera is attached to the bonnet of the car and my fellow actor and I have been sent off on our own round the block. We've had to use the slate ourselves to mark the take. They can then check it through the camera when we return.

You will certainly be meeting a low-loader at some point, that's for sure. A low-loader is a trailer that the car you're supposedly driving is set on. The trailer is low on the road, hence the name, so that to the viewer it looks as though your car is actually on the road itself.

A low-loader, courtesy of Action 99 Cars Ltd.

As you can see, the low-loader is towed by a camera truck (a truck with an open platform on the back), that the camera crew, director and script supervisor can sit on. This takes the pressure off you driving so you can concentrate on the dialogue and the scene. But there is a danger here: you may look like that's exactly what you're doing... *not* driving. In fact, I'd always prefer to be doing the driving, it keeps the scene more natural as you concentrate on one action, while playing another. There is a tendency to *act* driving on the low-loader, to turn the wheel too much, to be too busy: 'Look... I'm driving here.' The fact is, you don't turn a steering wheel that much when you drive: you're just watching the road. And what do you do when you're 'just watching'? Yes... *nothing.*

A low-loader from the actor's perspective.

You can certainly throw the odd flick of the eyes to the rearview and side mirrors, but that's all that's needed. You'll always have a walkie-talkie in the car, by the way, so that you can hear 'Action!' or discuss things with the director or operator.

It can be a bit throwing to have the whole camera crew and director in your direct eye-line, so think about where your looks are and pick an eye-line for the road, again remembering that your eyes are relatively static when driving.

I'm often aware, as a viewer, that the actor driving on what is obviously a low-loader spends a worrying amount of time looking at his/her fellow actor and not at the road. Always a bit of a give-away.

If you have a scene where you drive up and get out of a car, you'll have a mark to hit – this can be a bit tricky to get used to. Try to find something to your side: a gate, a lamp post, a door, anything that can give you a mark that's at eye level. It's not the easiest thing in the world to hit a mark with a car, so don't panic if you're not quite on it the first couple of times.

If you have to make a quick get-away, you can have the engine running before the take. They can easily remove the sound of the engine in post and add the sound of the car starting.

# HORSERIDING

Be careful not to say you can ride a horse when you can't. Okay, if you've plenty of time to get lessons before you start to shoot, but horses are dangerous to be on when you don't really know what you're doing and you're on a set... *and* you're trying to get a scene right!

# FOOD

Whatever level of production you're working on, you have to look after yourself, and this takes discipline and commitment. Filming can mean that you don't get much exercise. A lot of actors run, of course, which is terrific. When I get home after a day's work, I'll usually give myself a quick workout, fifteen to twenty minutes or so. This gives me a lift if I'm tired. Then I'll work on the next day's scenes, eat and relax – and get to bed early.

Talking of self-discipline, let's discuss *food*. Unless you're working in a studio on either television or a movie, you'll have catering. This means that when you arrive on location at say 6.30–7 a.m. there is breakfast available, and I mean the works: full English, whatever you fancy. Around mid-morning, coffee, tea and biscuits will be there, just off the set. Then lunch will offer a big selection, from salads to roast beef and Yorkshire pudding, fish and chips, whatever; and for desert, Black Forest gateau with cream or ice cream, spotted dick and custard, cheese and biscuits. Mid-afternoon: more biscuits, tea and coffee will appear. If you're working an extended day, till 8 or 9 p.m., say, there'll be soup or some pizza maybe around 7 p.m., to keep everyone going.

Now to a young, hungry actor this is a bit of a result... but beware! If you've had a good breakfast, biscuits and coffee through the morning and then devour a serious three-course lunch, you can find yourself drowsy and brain-dead by 3.30–4 p.m. You've got important close-ups to shoot, and you can barely stay awake! This is serious. Despite all my experience, I'll still find myself having jam roly-poly and custard, thinking, 'What the hell am I doing eating this? I never eat this!' But it's there. And therefore must be eaten! Breaking for lunch is essential in a long day, but there is always a post-lunch slump right across the unit as we all try to get back into the rhythm of the shoot. But for us actors, this is critical. Always be aware, when you do break, of what you're coming back to. Is it, in fact, your close-up, the most important part of your performance in any scene? Then you must keep that in your head over lunch. Try and eat just what you need: keep it simple and light if you can. Don't over-load yourself or your work could suffer.

**FOOD**

The one exception to this rule is Ms Helena Bonham Carter, who can eat for England when she's shooting, and constantly craves 'fuel'! But she always comes up with the goods and stays looking wonderful... Dammit!

On a soap, and other studio-bound productions, you may well be buying your own lunch from the canteen. At least there it's not free, but watch yourself nonetheless. On a studio-shot feature, you may be going to a canteen for lunch there too, but the same applies.

Sadly, colour film has the appearance of putting about 5lbs on your weight. Black-and-white film makes you look slimmer. Boy, those old Hollywood stars had it made: that beautiful lighting and in black and white!

By the way, I've been fortunate enough to shoot on two different features in France, and they have a wonderful and civilised system when you shoot in the studio. Instead of getting up at some ungodly hour, and trying to act at eight o'clock in the morning, you have a late breakfast or early lunch and don't start shooting till noon. You then shoot through until seven in the evening without a break. There is always food laid out so that you can grab a snack to keep you going, and, being French, it's delicious. It's a wonderful way to work: there's no after-lunch slump, and it's much more productive as a result. *'Vive la France!'* is all I can say.

# ADR

ADR is the only area of the post-production process that you will be directly involved in. You may well be called back a few weeks after you've wrapped to re-voice some of your dialogue. It's actually quite rare not to have to do this, and it's almost always for technical reasons. It could be traffic noise over lines in an exterior street scene or an aeroplane overhead. It's rarely to do with performance, but you can, in fact, alter the reading of a line in ADR to improve inflection and intention.

Looping, post-syncing or, as it's now called, ADR (Automatic Dialogue Replacement), is a process that I enjoy, but it can take a little getting used to. You may be sent the dialogue beforehand; if not, there will be a list of the lines to be re-recorded there on the day.

You'll turn up at a recording suite – they vary in size, from quite large at one of the major film studios like Pinewood, to really quite small in the heart of Soho. The director will be there, possibly the producer and two or three sound engineers, who specialise in mixing the sound in post-production. It's essentially an open studio with a large or small cinema screen or just a large monitor in it, with the technicians at a mixing desk behind you. There'll be some kind of stand to take your script pages (like a music stand), and you may well have a high stool to perch on if you fancy. I generally prefer standing since it keeps my energy up. You'll also have a pair of headphones to wear; I'd suggest you pull one off behind your ear so that you can hear your voice in a more natural way as you try to recreate your performance (there may only be one headphone anyway). There will be a mic on a stand and they will probably fit you with a throat mic as well.

You'll work in small chunks of dialogue, a line or two at a time. Watch the playback for each set of lines maybe two or three times. Judge this for yourself: if you need to watch it more than that, just ask. You won't feel any pressure from anyone in ADR. This is a much more relaxed process for the director: the pressure of the shoot is off them now. This may well be the first time you've seen footage of yourself in the role, but don't get caught up with judging your performance or what you look like – the picture will be ungraded in any case, i.e. the colours and tones haven't been finalised yet (in other words, you may not look your best). So concentrate on the job you're there to do.

Rehearse it for yourself. Try the dialogue out loud, along with the original, and get used to matching it exactly with your mouth. What you'll hear as the scene is played are three beeps, then fourth beep is your cue to start.

Simultaneously a white line passes from the left to the right of the screen, and as it hits the right-hand edge it'll be in sync with that fourth beep. So you have both an aural and a visual aid as your cue to begin your line.

Waiting for the white line to hit the right of the screen.

The aim is to match your original performance and get it perfectly in sync with your mouth movements. This seems tricky but you'll quickly get used to it. You may find there's a phrase or a line that you want to try in a different way from the original take. The director may suggest something, or it may occur to you on the spur of the moment. Remember, each time you try a line, that the recording will be kept so you can try a number of alternatives and they can use whatever seems best later in the sound mix. I might do my jumping-up-and-down business to get my adrenalin up to give certain lines some urgency, if that's required.

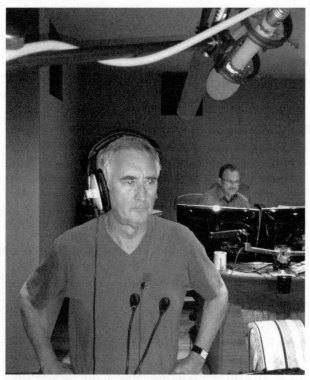

Only one headphone and a throat mic clipped to my T-shirt.

Going back to the French movie, *Providence*, Dirk Bogarde had to re-voice his entire role because the director Alain Resnais wasn't happy with the quality of the sound on the dialogue; it was a major role and days of work. Bogarde was not pleased.

When I worked with Burt Lancaster on *Local Hero*, there was a particular scene where he just couldn't get the lines right. 'There's always one,' he said. 'I'll do it in the loop.' Looping (as it used to be called, before digital technology got hold of it) was the same process as ADR but done on film itself; a loop of film would be put together for each line or lines from a scene, then run back and forward for each take. Lancaster stopped worrying about drying in the scene, said whatever came to mind then revoiced the dialogue properly in 'the loop'. This is a real movie actor's understanding of the process. He'd worked with Visconti in Italy where the actors who couldn't speak Italian would just say various numbers in English and then Italian actors would re-voice the dialogue in the loop. There was a long shot in *Local Hero* that Lancaster did with Fulton Mackay on the beach where they were both just saying numbers.

If you look at Lancaster in Visconti's *The Leopard*, or *A Fistful of Dollars* (and the other 'spaghetti westerns') with Clint Eastwood, directed by an Italian, Sergio Leone, it's all too obvious that this was happening!

It's not something I'd recommend in today's British film and television industry, but I do know that some major American movie actors are not averse to doing ADR on most of their performance, because they get paid a substantial amount for doing so!

I've certainly heard of some movie actors who can't remember lines or can't be bothered to learn them (believe it or not), who will either wear an earpiece and have their lines fed to them by someone holding the script or have 'idiot boards' (sometimes held by a fellow actor) with their lines written there. Marlon Brando was well known for using both these techniques. Now this can slow down a scene badly, but that lack of pace can be restored through ADR and the edit.

You can see how far away from that stage mentality and discipline you are in this world.

* * *

Here is a brief outline for each department's role in a film unit that I haven't already covered.

# THE PRODUCER

The role of the producer can be difficult to understand and hard to define. Producers are often the butt of actors' frustrations, but believe me it's a tough, stressful occupation. It takes a lot of nerve and tenacity, particularly as an 'independent', i.e. outside the major television companies; and even tougher as a freelance producer in features.

We'll take a look at the television industry first. In British television there are four main companies who commission drama: the BBC, Channel 4, ITV and Sky. They all work with independent producers as well as 'in-house' departments to develop original productions.

At the BBC, for instance, there's the Head of Drama Commissioning. He/she is in constant touch with the in-house departments and independent production companies looking for the best new shows to develop. Commissioning a project means that you are laying out finance to have a script written, which will then be assessed to see if it's a viable proposition to actually produce. If it gets the go-ahead, the term 'green-lit' is used to denote that the money will be released to actually make the programme. There are commissioning executives working for the drama commisioner who develop shows and represent the various regions, Scotland, Wales, Northern Ireland and England. There are also independent production companies who are doing the same thing and presenting projects to the major television channels.

Once a show has been green-lit, the executive producer will appoint a producer to actually make the programme. So the executive is actually in charge of the project, and the producer will be answerable to them.

The producer's job is to take the scripts and get them up and running. The first thing they'll do is get the director on board (there may be more than one if it's a six-parter or longer) and then start the casting process. Once that's happening, the producers start to talk to the designer about the look of the show. Any decisions about key personnel will have to be approved by the executive and the commissioner. The producer will be talking to the executive every day, and the exec will, in turn, be talking to the commissioner. The producer will then bring in a line producer who will administer the shoot itself: they will work very closely together. It's the line producer's job to make sure the shoot is within budget. They will have daily chats, and there will be fortnightly cost reports, which the exec will also see and comment on. Once rushes start coming in, the producer will be getting feedback from the exec and the commissioner and passing it on to the various departments on the production.

From an actor's perspective, the director in this scenario has less control than we might imagine (particularly in long-running series), but that's the way modern television functions.

The director generally has more control in the features world, where there are dozens of different situations. For instance, the project might have originated with the director, who brings it to a particular producer, but, broadly speaking, the same ground rules apply – except that there is no commissioner at the top of the tree. It's the executive producer who will take a project, raise the money, and bring in a director (if not already on board), producer and line producer, etc. Each feature, however, tends to be a one-off, so the various personalities involved will determine where the control lies for that particular project in terms of casting, choice of the various departments, and even who has final say in the actual editing process. You can't, for instance, imagine Steven Spielberg not being allowed final approval on casting and script changes on a film he's directing, but that may be a very different situation with a first-time features director. Using a first-time director can have an impact on the amount of money the executive can raise. In fact, if there's a big budget involved, the director may have to deal with a lot more interference from the producers than on a smaller one, but even here it really does come down to the personalities involved. There's a phrase, 'final cut', which is a contractual condition, and which would allow the director final say on the completed edit of his/her film. It is, in fact, very hard to achieve, and a director would need a pretty impressive track record to be allowed control over the final cut.

# THE PRODUCTION OFFICE

The line producer looks after the business management side of things. Along with the accountant on the unit, he/she keeps track of the budget as the production is running. A production manager works with and for the line producer and is answerable to them.

The line producer does have the facility to encompass the jobs of accountant, production manager and location manager. At one time in television all of those jobs were done by the line producer; nowadays things are structured differently, and the jobs are spread between these various departments.

In a movie there could be several production managers working for the line producer, one looking after the vehicle side of things, another construction, another with the design department, all organising and keeping track of their budget.

There is a budget for each department, and the line producer tries to keep everyone working within that budget, or they're manoeuvring money around between departments to keep the budget as a whole under control.

The line producer will also work with the 1st AD on the schedule; and with the location manager, checking on whether chosen locations are both practical and affordable. The parameters of the job can depend on what the producer requires, and how involved they might want to be in the detail. They may also be handling contracts. It's a collaboration. The line producer is in at the start of prep (pre-production) or earlier. It's the same role on a movie but bigger.

Within the production office there is also a production secretary and office assistants, the number depending on the size of the production.

# THE ART DEPARTMENT

The art director is responsible for the overall design of the sets for the production. This may involve building sets from scratch in a studio or adapting an existing building or rooms to fit the needs of the production. They will be working closely with the director to achieve the look and atmosphere of the piece. They will have assistants, the number again depending on the scale of the production.

The props buyer, props master and standby props work under the art director within this department. You will have daily contact with props as they magically appear with what you need for a particular scene. There will also be a standby art director, who will always be to hand if any problems come up.

The construction manager, carpenters, painters and stagehands are all involved in building sets from scratch or adapting existing buildings and rooms, under the direction of the art director.

# THE CASTING DEPARTMENT

The casting director will be working closely with the producer and director, during prep, before shooting starts, but also with some roles being cast during the shoot itself. Obviously, on a long-running series, the casting department are constantly looking for and meeting and auditioning actors.

Final casting approval, particularly of the principal roles, will be with the director, producer and the controller of whichever television network is involved, who will often having the most powerful voice.

In movies it can vary from production to production, depending on the size of the budget, but even low-budget films will be looking for some kind of 'name' or 'names' to hang the publicity on. On big-budget movies those 'names' become really critical.

# THE CATERERS

The caterers are up at some ungodly hour and working before the crew and cast get to the location; producing breakfast and lunch for sixty or more out of the back of a trailer. They usually wrap a bit before the rest of the unit unless, of course, the day's shoot goes into the evening. Then they have to get back to wherever their base is and stock up for first thing the next morning. One thing is for sure, an army marches on its stomach and so does a film crew. Good caterers can really keep the morale and energy of the unit up, just as bad ones can have the opposite effect. There have been rare occasions when I've started bringing my own food in rather than suffer the depression of a bad lunch. A very important department!

# THE EDITOR

I can't stress what a massive impact an editor can have on a production. They bring such a huge contribution not just to the pace and energy of a piece but to the whole style in which it's presented. A lot of modern cinema is dominated by very fast cutting to keep the audience gripped and excited. This is very obvious in an 'action movie': just watch one from the point of view of the number of cuts that are happening from shot to shot. It can be so fast. From an actor's perspective, this means that quite often only fragments of our performance are seen at a time, because it's all to do with narrative drive, a very American obsession. By the way, I'm not being disparaging here: it's a stylistic choice like any other.

At the other end of the scale are slower-paced, more conventionally shot movies, more character-driven. The style and pace of a piece is, of course, very much in the director's hands, but the editor is there to realise the director's vision and to add his/her contribution. So, the editor works very closely with the director: on a movie this relationship varies according to the way the director likes to work. The editor may well be cutting scenes together through the shoot, with the director dropping in at the end of a day's work, to check how it's coming together, or perhaps leaving things for a few days and seeing what the editor has come up with, or maybe looking at the takes for that day and making notes and comments about which takes he/she wants the editor to use. The director also gives notes on takes to the script supervisor who then passes on to the editor. The producer may well be keeping an eye on the edit too.

An editor can actually improve a performance that is weak or mar one that is brilliant. Comedy is very interesting from the point of view of the editor. Timing and pace is crucial in their hands, which is, after all, the essence of comedy.

The real work on the edit will happen in post. This is, hopefully, a much calmer time for the director as the pressure of the shoot has gone; and mostly it'll just be the director and the editor working quietly together. Of course, on those big movies the producers may be in and out looking at how it's taking shape and making comments – which can put the director and the editor under a lot of pressure.

As in 'More Money, More Time' (see pages 24–26), television can be a much faster process for the editor and, therefore, the director. On a soap like *EastEnders*, or on *Holby City* and *Casualty*, the edit, sound-mix and grade are going on during the shoot as it's possible some of these shows could be transmitting within five days of shooting. The producers on these types of productions have a lot of control, which can mean a corresponding lack of control for the director.

*New Tricks* has four weeks of editing time for two one-hour episodes. A four-part drama would have roughly the same, i.e. a ninety-minute drama would have between five to six weeks to edit, and a two-hour piece between seven to eight weeks.

As you move into drama series, say a six-parter or one-off dramas (quite rare these days), there's more time for the editor and director to spend together, to fine-tune what's been shot.

Going back to movies, it's really dependent on the budget, but on a big Hollywood action picture you're looking at many times more than those television schedules for the edit and post-production.

# HEALTH AND SAFETY

The fact is that film sets can be dangerous places: lights hanging from rigging, lights on stands, tracks on the ground, cables on the ground. Even the camera that you're standing so close to for your off-lines can suddenly pan and hit you, so be aware of your head and your feet.

# UNIT NURSE

There should always be a unit nurse on a shoot. He/she can deal with anything from a cold to you falling over a track or getting hurt in action (a chase or a fight). Even if it's only fatigue from a heavy schedule, they'll have a good supply of Berocca or something similar (other brands are available).

# LIGHTING

The gaffer works pretty closely with the DOP, making sure he can achieve what's required from a technical point of view, with the sparks working under him. There is always a generator on location, which has a genny operator with it. This needs to be parked somewhere so that no noise impinges on the set.

You don't see many females in lighting departments, but there's no reason they couldn't be there. The unit does tend to be a very male-dominated world. The best boy, by the way, is the assistant to the gaffer, so second in the chain of command in the lighting department.

# MUSIC

The composer is, of course, a vital element in any production, and the scale and ambition of their work is very much at the mercy of the budget, i.e. can they afford that full orchestral sound? Or do they have to achieve what they want electronically or scale it down using a simpler acoustic sound? These days so much can be achieved in the recording studio at a minimum of cost.

They too are working very closely with the director, contributing so much to the final mood, atmosphere and pace of the piece. At the same time, you don't want the music to dominate the film. Most of the time it should be subliminal, unless, of course, there are opportunities for a big musical impact.

On big television series they may well be coming up with a theme tune and a style of music which could be used for years on a long-running series.

Going back to Miles Davis, he scored a French movie in the fifties, *Lift to the Scaffold*, with his band improvising to sections of the movie in the studio.

# STILLS PHOTOGRAPHER

There will always be a stills photographer attached to the unit. They'll usually come and say hello; if not, say hello to them. I don't usually like having stills shot during a take. If I'm aware of another lens poking at me, apart from the camera, I find it very distracting. I want my sole concentration on the lens that's taking my performance. I'll mention this to the stills photographer when we say hello. They can shoot during rehearsals, or they can set up some shots when there's a break. It's quite a pressured job on stills, to get in there and get some good shots with very little time and opportunity.

Even after all these years I find set-up stills a bit difficult. I guess you have to come out of character for them, so it's just you. It can be useful to run a bit of dialogue while being photographed, so you're more in there and less self-conscious.

# POST-PRODUCTION SUPERVISOR

The post-production supervisor is the person who looks after all aspects of the post-production process, once principal photography is completed. They will work out the post-production schedule, organise ADR and ensure the picture grading and dubbing are ready as needed, to meet contractual delivery dates.

# POST-PRODUCTION SCRIPTS AND DELIVERY

The post-production script is a fresh copy of the script, which is put together after the shoot has finished. Whoever is supervising this will sit down with the final cut of the production on DVD and the script, and painstakingly go through it, writing a fresh draft with any cuts or additions to the dialogue that have occurred during the shoot.

There will also be accurate notes on where any music comes in. If there's music other than that specially composed for the piece, i.e. music that's already recorded, say pop tracks, how much was paid for those tracks? This can be an expensive outlay if they're well known. This is known as 'getting clearance'; it can be a big issue for the budget, paying for the right to use certain tracks.

In television this final draft is passed on to the broadcaster for use with overseas sales. Whichever country buys the programme will get this script as well so that they can add subtitles or indeed re-voice it in their own language. If the programme is an hour long (on the BBC that's actually fifty-eight to fifty-nine minutes) it will be cut down to fifty minutes for overseas sales so that commercials can be inserted. So you might find that some of your favourite moments have hit the cutting-room floor in Spain or Florida.

There will also be a list of actors' fees so that any residual payments (a percentage of your original fee) can be passed on to you. This will also include the composer. The same would apply in features, with the script being held by the production company.

# CLEARENCE AND LEGAL

The clearance and legal team ensure that the contracts for both crew and cast include all the elements required: finance agreements for partners (other companies who are jointly financing the project), percentage splits for the 'back end' profits, exploitation rights for DVD sales, the agreement for film finances should the production run into financial trouble, location agreements, etc.

The 'back end', by the way, is basically after the movie/television production has covered its costs and goes into profit. There are occasions where actors may (if their profile is sufficiently high) get a piece of the 'back end', or there might be a situation where, because the budget for a particular movie is on the low side, an actor may agree to a smaller fee than usual but take a piece of the 'back end'. I've only every heard of this in features, not in television.

# INSURANCE

Production insurance is usually based on a percentage of the total costs, to cover claims for an artist being unable to work on any given day, damage to locations and equipment, etc. Insuring against the weather is so expensive that it's not considered. In a sense, insurance is like your car or house, and covers normal eventualities.

# SITUATION COMEDY (SITCOM)

As I write that phrase, I wonder why? What the hell does it mean? A 'comedy' which is set in a 'situation'? I guess at base it means a studio-bound comedy with few sets: it tends to be mostly in one location and explores the same basic 'situation' in each episode.

In any event, sitcom is a strange hybrid of a thing, because you're working with cameras and an audience at the same time. This is all Lucille Ball's fault. Or to be more accurate, her husband's, Desi Arnaz. In life, as in the show, he was a bandleader who played opposite Lucille, and it was he who introduced not just the audience but a multi-camera set-up (they were film cameras then) into the studio in 1951.

*I Love Lucy* was massively successful through the fifties, not least because Lucille Ball was the most superb comedienne. If you've never seen it, I'd highly recommend that you do. She was a big influence on me, I've nicked a few gags from her in my time, but, to be quite frank, she's left us all with a bit of a handful.

Let me first of all take you through the mechanics of the working process. Unlike most film work, you have a rehearsal period. A sitcom is never longer than half an hour. You're dealing with very specific timings here: the programme length is twenty-nine minutes on BBC 1 and 2, twenty-eight minutes on BBC 3, with trailers and credits at either end. On the commercial channels, it's twenty-four minutes: they have trailers and commercials at either end and, of course, a commercial break in the middle, so each half is twelve minutes. This may vary but only by very little; you certainly wouldn't be allowed to go over that thirty-minute format on any channel. On the commercial side they'll want to construct the script with a nice punchy gag or some kind of comic cliffhanger at the end of the first half. In a sense it's like an extended sketch, and it takes great skill to write, direct and *act* the damn thing!

You'll generally rehearse for five days, working from around 10.30 a.m. till 1.30 p.m., in a rehearsal room. This might vary if you're doing a pilot, where you'll need more time to get a new idea into shape. The half-day rehearsal gives you the chance to work on the lines in the afternoon. The floor is marked out with white gaffer tape, to denote dimensions of rooms, positions of doors, etc. This is done by the stage manager, who on the studio day will be responsible for any props used and anything else they can help the floor manager with. The floor manager (who'll be in to rehearsals at some point) is like a 1st AD on a film unit; he/she is in charge of the studio floor. The director will by then be in the control room, and the floor manager will run the studio day for the director. At that point there will also be a floor Assistant and any number of runners.

You'll start, as normal, with a readthrough. I'm not generally that keen on readthroughs but this case is different: here, due to the tight schedule, I want as much exposure to the script as possible. Then come rehearsals with the director. There can be quite a lot of script changes coming at you over these days as you work on and fine-tune the script, with ideas coming from the director, the producer and the writers, and some from the actors themselves. In this country there's usually only one writer, but occasionally there can be a team of writers on one show, an idea that's grown out of the American approach, as was the case with *My Family*. Coping with late changes can put pressure on you when you know that you have to step in front of an audience in two or three days.

There may well be scenes that demand to be shot on location and replayed to the audience during the studio day. Of course, the more scenes you shoot like this, the less pressure on the day itself.

On the last day of rehearsals or towards the end of the week, you'll do a producer's run: you may have various technicians present or they may drop in through the week. This gives the run a bit of a lift, and can cause some nerves, but it's all useful since you'll be hitting the audience in the next day or so. It's very possible that there could be script changes after the producers have been in, but hopefully they'll not be too extensive.

Another variation is to rehearse for three full days, then have a full day in the studio, probably without cameras, then on the fifth and final day as normal, with a camera rehearsal, then the audience. This would mean they have a bigger budget because that extra studio day is expensive.

# THE STUDIO DAY

Sitcom is a multi-camera set-up, using three to five cameras simultaneously. It can be a bit tricky keeping track of which camera you are on at any given moment. However, on the studio day, a camera script will be in circulation; this contains a detailed breakdown of each shot through the recording. You'll see terms opposite dialogue like:

- **CU** (close-up): the bottom of the frame is at your collar or chest.

- **BCU** (big close-up): the bottom of the frame is at your chin.

- **Mid-shot**: bottom of the frame is around waist height.

- **Wide shot**: your full body is in frame, right to the floor.

- **Two-** to **five-shot**: from two to five actors are in the same frame.

There are certain directors who will depart from the camera script and vary things on the day in terms of shots.

Now if you're a novice and you want to let all this go and just concentrate on your performance, that's absolutely fine, but as you gain more experience, the camera script can be a great help. You will also develop a 'third eye' for the telltale red light that appears on top of the camera that's actually recording – you can keep track of the shots that way *and* remember your lines *and* be *funny*!

You'll notice that most sitcoms are rather brightly lit. This has a lot to do with the fact that enough light has to be thrown across the set to accommodate all the cameras involved. It's also a stylistic television choice, to present an upbeat, bright image to help the comedy. Sadly it doesn't always do the actors' faces any favours, though this is improving with better lighting along with HD, which has taken over in this arena as well, replacing the terrible DigiBeta cameras we've struggled with for so many years.

The studio day is a long one, starting around 9.30–10 a.m. You begin with a camera rehearsal on the sets, with the cameras strung out along the length of the studio open towards the audience.

This is not usually done in costume, but if you want to wear it, that shouldn't be a problem. The camera rehearsal is a long, slow process, not unlike a technical rehearsal in the theatre. The director will be in the control room working through the shots. He/she will have a vision mixer on one side, and on the other, the script supervisor, who will be calling the shots out. These are vital personnel for the director, as is the floor manager.

You'll work through each scene, adjusting positions for the shots, then probably run that scene before moving on. You'll break for lunch around 1 p.m. for an hour, then work on till 4.30–5 p.m., at which point you'll break, do costume and make-up, then do a dress run with the cameras, running the whole show as a performance, with any previously shot location scenes slotted in. It's possible that you may also pre-record a scene during the studio day itself, which cuts into your studio time.

You'll then take a break for an hour and a half or so before recording the show with the audience at around 7.30 p.m. There are occasions, owing to time pressures, that you don't have a dress at all.

One of the challenges of this way of working is that by the time you get to the audience, you can be just a bit knackered. Television studios are large, black, airless boxes that can really sap your energy. Be aware of the day ahead and try to pace yourself.

# THE ACTUAL RECORDING

If you want to see the studio in operation, watch the BBC sitcom *Mrs Brown's Boys*. It has shots of the studio sets and audience at the top and tail of each show; a brilliant deconstruction of the fourth wall.

About twenty minutes or so before the recording starts, a warm-up man will be talking to the audience, throwing well-rehearsed gags at them, encouraging them to participate and generally getting them... 'warmed up'. A good warm-up man is invaluable: if he's not funny enough or makes the audience uncomfortable, that's not going to help you; on the other hand, a warm-up man who's too good can be also be a liability. If he's too funny, making the audience laugh too much, he'll a) make them tired, and b) make *you* look less funny than he is – that you do not want!

Many years ago when Robert Lindsay was recording an episode of *Citizen Smith*, the floor manager came to him before the recording and told him to get out to the studio fast because the warm-up man had the audience in hysterics. When Bob got out there he found the warm-up man standing on his head, reading the news in Australian – follow that! By the way, that warm-up man was Michael Barrymore.

Just before we start to record, all the cast will assemble backstage, immediately behind the set, while on stage the floor manager, the producer or warm-up man will announce each actor in turn – this is everyone, by the way, both the leads and supporting roles. When you are called, you'll walk out, smile, wave and try to look relaxed! Then go to your first position, or walk back off for your first entrance. Some leading actors may have a quick chat to the audience at this point; on rare occasions they may even do their own warm-up.

And so to the recording...

This is a stop/start affair: of course, everyone wants it to go as smoothly as possible, but things may well go wrong, either with the actors or technically. The tricky area here is laughter; we want lots of laughs, but if we're repeating gags too often, the audience will find them less and less funny. Their laughter is being recorded on a separate track – you'll notice mics strung along the length of the seating – so that in the edit, 'laughter' can be moved around and dropped in here and there. There have certainly been series recorded without an audience, and with a stock laughter track dropped in during the edit, but this is never satisfactory and can be very irritating for the viewer. It also lacks that spontaneous 'atmosphere' that the live audience brings.

When I was doing the comedy series, *The Kit Curran Radio Show*, we used to build a 'mistake' into the first scene of the recording each week: we'd stop and utter some mild expletive, then laugh with the audience at our own mistake. This had the effect of breaking the ice, as it were, letting the audience 'in' on the show.

One of the tricky aspects of the studio day is that the kind of audience who turn up to see the recording of a show like this tend to be less sophisticated and to prefer broader humour. If you're not careful you can end up 'mugging' and pushing gags in a way that may not suit the camera, or the audience at home, who may be a little more discerning. There can be occasions when you might get too much laughter and have to push on through with the dialogue, in a way you wouldn't in the theatre, where you'd wait for the wave of laughter to be just passing its peak before moving on. To be crude about it: if you mention 'tits', 'bum' 'knickers' or 'bastard', you may well get an overreaction, a bit 'end of the pier', which won't necessarily reflect the audience at home, so it's better to drive on through. Remember that you're working with microphones too, so you'll be heard okay over the audience. There are no throat mics here, by the way, it's always mics on booms.

You may find that you are vocally stronger than you might be on film, because of the theatricality of the set-up. This is quite normal.

The late, great Victor Spinetti once described the playing style in sitcom as 'floating two inches off the ground' (in other words, just slightly heightened). This is a perfect description as far as I'm concerned. There are some exceptions, sitcoms in which the playing style and pitch are still pretty naturalistic. Zoë Wanamaker in *My Family* is a very good example, as were Judi Dench and Geoffrey Palmer in *As Time Goes By*, but these are the exceptions rather than the rule.

Here is the essence of the challenge with this type of work: yes, I have an audience, but I'm also playing on the camera, so where is my focus? In the end it has to be for the camera, but you're juggling both elements, and it's bloody tricky. It's undeniable, though, that the energy and adrenalin that the audience brings to the equation does raise your game.

Usually the recording will take two to two-and-a-half hours; ideally it should finish within two hours because you'll risk the audience getting tired. You'll be a bit wiped out after it, but tomorrow's a day off... Well not quite – you'll probably have to start working on the next script. In the UK we tend not to do long 'seasons', as they do in the States. Six episodes would be normal; perhaps eight to ten for a second series of a successful sitcom. Being a leading actor in that situation is terrific but a lot of pressure. At one time I had my own comedy series, *The Kit Curran Radio Show*, doing six episodes, while carrying a West End show, *Lend Me a Tenor* (a high-energy farce), eight times a week... *never again*!

# PERFORMANCE CAPTURE

Motion tracking or motion capture started as a photogrammetric analysis tool in biomechanics research in the seventies and eighties, and expanded into education, training, sports and recently computer animation for television, cinema and video games as the technology matured. A performer wears markers near each joint to identify the motion by the positions or angles between the markers.

Performance capture is another level up from motion capture. As yet, I've not had direct experience of this technology so I spent some time with Andy Serkis at

The Imaginarium, the studio he runs with producer Jonathan Cavendish at Ealing Studios.

At The Imaginarium, they have 100 motion cameras in the studio, but you need to forget any notion of conventional cameras and lenses. These motion-capture cameras fire out beams in a similar way to lasers, that track objects in 3D space in relation to all the other cameras, and then can map out the world in the software. If this is all a bit much to wrap your head around, don't worry, because from the actor's point of view, this can be a very liberating experience.

It certainly demands the same level of preparation and emotional commitment as a 'normal' performance, but you are given the opportunity to play roles that you would never get near because your physical shape and size can be manipulated to any degree from tiny to huge – but it is still *your* performance.

In short: this technology should be embraced and savoured.

142

As you can see from the photograph, you are wearing a kind of 'jumpsuit' covered in body markers, which are used to track the motions of the body in the performance-capture software. For facial capture there are two options – either head-mounted cameras (HMCs)...

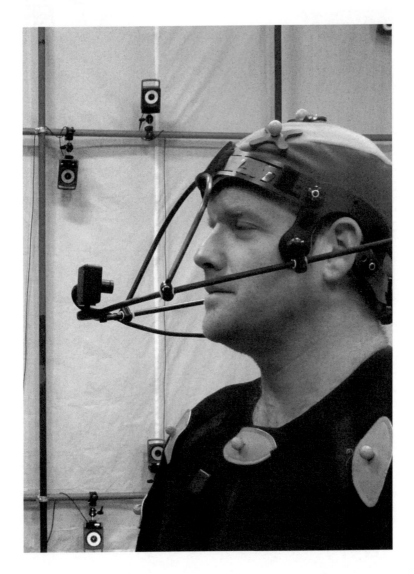

...or optical facial capture – which is where markers are applied to the face with make-up.

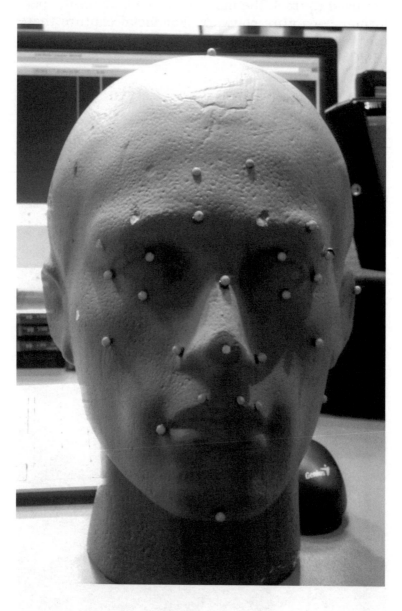

Additional detail and weights can be added to the suits in order to achieve the desired movement for your character. For example, as a heavy-footed troll, you'd need some feet weights to move in the required way.

You're not working blind here; you will have a monitor in front of you as you start to work so you can see the 'real-time rig' (the character they've manipulated your image in to), be it a dragon or a tiny elf. This is not a fully rendered result but a basic animation showing how the character moves in real time, in order to pre-visualise the piece. Character technical directors will design this rig beforehand so you can see it moving in sync whilst you act. There are specifically designed motion-capture cameras all around you, gathering 360 degrees of data, recording continuously.

Before you start to record you'll do a 'range of motion' (ROM), in order to give the performance-capture system the extremes of your movements so it can build your skeleton.

The studio is essentially a white box; there is no need for a set – that can be created by computer. The bare bones of any furniture will be used, a box for an armchair, for instance. The armchair design will be made beforehand and put into the real-time environment. The day I was watching, a simple box on the floor became a sumptuous armchair. Props work in a similar way – a plank of wood can be made into a sword in the real-time system.

You'll work with the director and block the scene as normal, then do a camera rehearsal. Apart from the cameras surrounding the action there is also a 'virtual camera' that can be tracked or hand-held.

Once the scene is shot in the 360-degree space, the actors can step out and the director can do all the close-ups and other shots he/she wants with the virtual camera. On the real-time screen, which the director can see through the virtual camera, the actors appear to still be there, performing their scene. Different directors choose to shoot performance capture in different ways – some frame their shots through real-time, with the actors playing out the scenes over a few takes, but some do all their takes in the wide, and then the actors leave and the director can frame the shots afterwards, using the virtual camera.

The benefit of this is that you can get on a roll in performance doing many takes without the constant technical interruptions of a normal shoot.

Lighting can be manipulated in any direction; scenes can be plunged into deep shadow or transformed to bright daylight on computer.

You can therefore work much faster than is normally possible, with a greater sense of freedom. Andy's team were about to shoot a ninety-minute performance-capture feature in eight weeks.

The actors I talked to on the day, including Andy, said that you forget very quickly about what you are wearing, including the headgear, and sink yourself into the scene and the role. They are working on developing less intrusive headgear with smaller cameras for the head mount, that would sit either side of the face to get even more detail, possibly progressing to four.

The games industry also use performance capture, and one of the aims for the future is to have interactive drama where the viewer can not only control the storyline, but ultimately enter and be part of the action itself, perhaps with the aid of some sort of virtual visor.

With this technology it would be possible to scan and record actors and use them, without them needing to be there, even after they've died. We could have Ian McKellen around in fifty to a hundred years' time still doing *The X-Men* or *The Hobbit*!

Here's a quote from Benedict Cumberbatch about the experience of motion capture on *The Hobbit*:

I was mainly on my belly on the floor playing at being a dragon. It was like being a kid: no marks, no make-up, no continuity, no worries about camera positions. It was so much fun.

# THERE ARE NO RULES

One of the fascinations of our job is that you're always changing; you're picking up different ideas from each part, using them in the next; discovering, discarding, retrying. My own feelings and theories about my work fluctuate and develop as I progress, and that's as it should be. Which leads me onto... *there are no rules...* and if you learn some as you go along, it's always worth breaking them to see what happens.

Here's a couple of examples. As I began to work with film scripts, I'd prepare them in a linear way. This helps to counteract the fact that you're shooting out of sequence. You could be shooting the last moments of your character's journey at the beginning of the schedule (it's not ideal, of course, but it does happen). I've even had instances of shooting an individual scene out of sequence (which is a bit tough). So I'd always work the script through and through, building up the development of the character in my head, so that I knew where and how my character was at any point in the narrative. I'd always want to know the scene before and the scene after the one we were shooting, so that I knew not only where I'd been, but also where I was going.

I saw an interview with the celebrated Russian film director Andrei Tarkovsky some years ago (among several other wonderful movies, he wrote and directed *Solaris*), where he talked about wanting his actors to only play the scene they were shooting, to take no notice of the narrative, but to play 'like children'. Now he might have been a patronising, controlling arsehole, I've no idea, but I came across this particular role in a single film for the BBC called *One Way Out*; he was a violent psychotic who was very unpredictable, and I decided to try Mr Tarkovsky's approach. I threw aside any notion of narrative and played each scene in isolation and, I guess, without motivation. I'd made plenty of decisions about who he was, his background, parents, etc., but never asked 'Why?' in each scene – I just *did*. I felt it was a very successful performance, and believe me I'm as self-critical as the next actor.

As I've said, I have a total aversion to stage directions, but when I played a character who suffered from obsessive compulsive disorder, there wasn't a huge amount of dialogue for him but there were a lot of stage directions. I decided not to ignore them or scrub them out, as is my wont, but to follow them slavishly, to the letter – compulsively, in fact. I've never done it since, but it was a great way into that particular part.

This is, I guess, not exactly within the remit of this book, but I feel it's worth mentioning...

# THE PRESS

If you have a movie or television programme coming out, you're going to be asked to do a certain amount of press for it. We've been made all too aware recently about the intrusion of the media into the lives of actors and other 'personalities', but frankly, not doing interviews is a very difficult thing to achieve these days.

However, you do have some choices. If you don't want to talk to certain tabloids, you can make this clear to the publicity department, and if there is the odd television chat show you'd rather not do, that can also be acceptable.

But here is a definite no-no: *never* allow a journalist into your home, for either an interview or to be photographed. It will feel like a real invasion.

*Never* have lunch or dinner with a journalist: you can find yourself at some very plush restaurant being wined and dined over a period of two hours or more, and you'll end up talking about personal stuff that you'll really regret.

When you do meet a journalist, do it on neutral ground – a café is fine – but make it clear that you've only got an hour at the very most. An office situation or a hotel that the production arranges is better, if that's achievable. A journalist will be looking for a 'hook' for an interview, some personal thing, a revelation preferably, that they can hang the interview on. If they know anything about you, they will have made up their mind about that hook before they meet you and try to steer you towards that.

Try not to give any details of your private life at all, at any time in your career: keep it work orientated. This can be very difficult. You don't want to be rude or confrontational, but believe me, once that stuff is out there, it's out there for all time! 'I'm sorry but I hate talking about my private life' should do the trick. Then you'll be known as 'that actor who never talks about their private life... Ooh, fascinating!' If they want a hook, there it is. 'The mysterious Denis Lawson...' sounds quite good (would it were true!).

It's generally easier doing a chat show on television, or on radio. The trouble with press interviews is that they can be doctored, changed, slanted in the way that the journalist/editor wants them to go. The reader doesn't know what the journalist asked, only what you 'seem' to have said. There are also blatant mistakes in reporting,

149

and then there are blatant lies too. The exception to this is where the article is published in a question-and-answer format.

I do wonder if, in fact, a lot of press and television interviews have a detrimental effect on our work. The audience comes to your performance with a received opinion about you, and it can therefore be harder to convince them that you are someone else. It's better if we retain a neutral image which we can then manipulate in our work. There are a couple of well-known actor friends of mine who have managed to go through pretty well their entire career having barely given an interview at all. Quite an achievement. It can be very flattering to the ego when the press first start taking an interest in you, but be wary: be very, very careful with yourself.

# KEEPING IT GREEN

There is a tremendous amount of waste on most film units. You'll come in first thing to your trailer and find all the lights on and a heater blasting away. There are also make-up and wardrobe trailers, and the camera truck. You could easily have twenty or so trailers (many more on a big feature) sucking all the energy from the generator. When you leave your trailer, remember to switch off all the lights – it's simple enough but rarely done, so all of those vehicles are using energy that's totally unnecessary while we're all on set.

You make yourself a cup of tea or coffee. It's a polystyrene cup and a plastic spoon that's then thrown away. Take your own mug in and use it through the day. There are loads of small plastic bottles of water being doled out all day to whoever needs them. Make sure that your initials are on your bottle so that you can keep track of it and it doesn't end up getting thrown away half-drunk.

# . . . AND IN CONCLUSION

So that's it and that's all, folks. The best way to finish this book is to tell you to re-read the *important notice* at the beginning.

Remember, this is my shit, that's all I can give you. Even if you just use this as a point of departure, I'm happy. At least now you have somewhere to depart from.

So depart, go forth, multiply too, if you fancy; but for God's sake, enjoy yourself along the way! I hope this book will help you to do just that.

# THANKS

I'd like to thank the following people for their invaluable help in the preparation of this book:

DOP Robin Vidgeon, for his patience and good humour while answering a stream of queries from me – several times over! And Tony Dowe, for his help on situation comedy.

The production team and crew on *New Tricks*, including Ian Scaiffe (line producer), Peter Sinclair (DOP), Julia Duff and Sacha Green (casting), and Amanda Searle (stills) for the cover photograph.

Brian Grant for the photographs in the section on ADR, Actions 99 Cars Ltd for the photographs of the low-loader, Ben Keene at Cloud12, and Spotlight.

Andy Serkis, Jonathan Cavendish, Catherine Slater and all at The Imaginarium Studios.

Phoebe Fox, Sharon Huff, Jo Joyner, Vincent Riotta, Magdalena Rodriguez, Lydia Wilson and Andrew Byatt.

And all the crews I've worked with throughout my career, for their focus and commitment.

*D.L.*